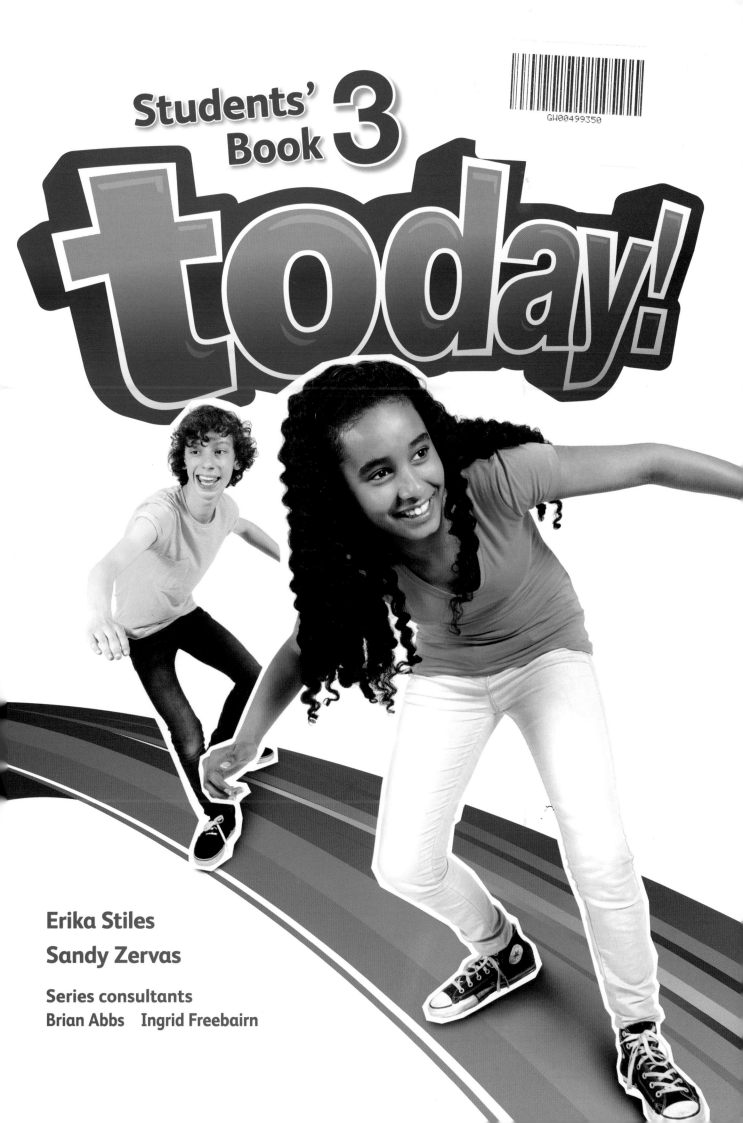

Students'
Book **3**

today!

Erika Stiles

Sandy Zervas

Series consultants
Brian Abbs   Ingrid Freebairn

GW00499350

Contents

1 On the move

Lesson aims:
- talk about appearance and personality
- talk about routines
- talk about things happening now

A I live in Chicago.

Rockport Academy
CHICAGO, USA

Write to your host family. Introduce yourself and write about:
- where you live
- your family
- what you do in your free time

USA UK Exchange Programme

Host family: Mr and Mrs Jones, Cambridge, UK

Dear Mr and Mrs Jones,

My name is Tom Harper. I'm thirteen and I go to Rockport Academy in Chicago.

My family and I live in Beverly, a suburb of Chicago. My dad is a doctor. He works in a children's hospital and he's very <u>hard-working</u>.

My mum makes birthday cakes and sells them. She's really creative and she's patient too. Right now, she's making a pirate ship cake! She works from home but she never works at weekends.

My brother, Greg, is older than me. He's a bit bossy but I don't mind. He's very clever and he wants to be a web designer. He's at college so he isn't living at home at the moment.

In my free time, I usually play basketball. I'm good but I'm not very tall! I'm sending you photos of me and my family with this letter. I've got dark curly hair but my brother's got straight fair hair.

I'm really looking forward to staying with you.

Yours sincerely,

Tom Harper

Presentation

1 (1 02) Listen and read. Which country is Tom from?

Comprehension

2 Read again and write *Tom (T)*, *Mum (M)*, *Dad (D)* or *Greg (G)*.

Who ...
1 is thirteen?
2 goes to college? ☐
3 likes making cakes? ☐
4 is a doctor? ☐
5 is creative? ☐
6 works with children? ☐

Memory check: Appearance

3 Describe Tom and his family. Use the words in the box or other words you know.

Hair:	curly	dark	fair	long	straight
Age:	old	young			
Size:	short	slim	tall		
General:	attractive	good-looking			

Tom is thirteen. He's got ... . He's ... .
Greg is ...

Vocabulary: Personality adjectives

4 **03** Listen and repeat. Which adjectives are in the text in Exercise 1? Find and underline them. Who do they describe?

bossy	cheerful	clever	creative	generous
grumpy	hard-working	honest	lazy	
patient	polite	rude	selfish	shy sociable

hard-working – Dad

5 Describe the people below. Use the adjectives in Exercise 4.

1 *He's cheerful.*

Grammar

Present simple

I <u>usually</u> **play** basketball in my free time.

Mum <u>never</u> **works** at weekends.

We **live** in Chicago.

We **don't live** in New York.

What **do** you **do** in your free time?

Present continuous

<u>Right now</u>, Mum **'s making** a pirate ship cake!

Greg **isn't living** at home <u>at the moment</u>.

What **are** you **doing** <u>now</u>?

6 Complete the letter from Dylan Jones. Use the present simple or present continuous.

Hi Tom,

Thanks for your letter. Here's a photo of my family at home in Cambridge. We ¹ *'re all smiling* (all smile)!

My mum is a teacher. She ² .... (teach) Art at our school. Dad is an engineer. Tara, my sister, is very bossy. She ³ .... (stand) next to Mum. She ⁴ .... (not sing) in the photo but she ⁵ .... (usually sing) all day! She goes to choir practice every day. The girl in the green T-shirt is her friend, Fran. She ⁶ .... (live) next door but she ⁷ .... (be always) at our house!

I ⁸ .... (love) computers and science. Unfortunately, I ⁹ .... (not know) much about basketball because we ¹⁰ .... (never play) it at my school. ¹¹ .... (you/ know) anything about rugby? That's my favourite sport. We're really looking forward to meeting you!

Best wishes,

Dylan Jones

Speaking

7 Ask and answer about the Jones family.

1 **A:** *Where do they live?*

   B: *They live in Cambridge.*

1 Where / they / live?

2 What / Mr and Mrs Jones / do?

3 What / Dylan and Tara / do / in their free time?

4 What / they / do / in the photo?

About you

8 A student from another country is coming to stay with your family. Write and tell him/her about your family. Use the letter in Exercise 6 to help.

> Now turn to Unit 1A in the Activity Book.

B When's Tom arriving?

Lesson aims:
· talk about transport and travel
· talk about future arrangements

Presentation

1 🔘 **Listen and read. Choose the correct words.**

Dylan: Mum, remind me. When's Tom arriving?

Tara: *(singing)*

Dylan: Tara, ssh! Stop singing for a moment! I'm talking to Mum!

Tara: Don't be so ¹(bossy)/ *lazy*!

Mrs Jones: Tom's arriving next week, on 3rd September.

Dylan: That's next ² *Tuesday / Thursday*. What time?

Mrs Jones: His plane lands at 10.05.

Tara: Cool. Are we meeting him at the airport?

Mr Jones: Yes, we are. We're going by car.

Tara: Can Fran come, too, Dad?

Mr Jones: Sorry, but I don't think there's ³ *lots of / enough* room. There's you, Dylan, your mum, me, Tom and lots of luggage. After all, he's staying for ⁴ *three / two* months.

Mrs Jones: Well, I want to cook a nice welcome lunch for him, anyway. Fran can go in my place.

Tara: Thanks, Mum!

Dylan: OK, but Tara, please, do us a favour?

Tara: Sure, what?

Dylan: Please don't ⁵ *talk / sing* all the way to the airport!

2 🔘 **Listen and repeat the dialogue.**

English today

· Remind me.
· Don't be so (bossy)!
· After all, …
· …, anyway.
· Please do (us) a favour.
· Sure, what?

Comprehension

3 **Read again and answer *True* (*T*) or *False* (*F*). Correct the false statements.**

1 Tara's singing loudly. [T]

2 Tom's arriving on 10th September. [F]
   Tom's arriving on 3rd September.

3 Tom's travelling to the UK by plane. ☐

4 The Jones family can't meet Tom at the airport. ☐

5 Tom's bringing a lot of luggage with him. ☐

6 Mr Jones is cooking dinner on Thursday. ☐

Memory check: Transport

4 **Match the words with the descriptions.**

boat	bus	car	coach	helicopter	plane
underground train					

1 They've got four wheels. *bus, car, coach*

2 We use them for air travel.

3 We use it for sea travel.

4 It runs under the city.

Vocabulary: Travel expressions

5 🔘 **Listen and repeat. Look at the pictures. What's Tom doing? Ask and answer.**

arrive – leave
catch – miss (the bus/plane)
check in – collect (your luggage)
get on – get off (the bus/train)
go through security
show (your passport)
take off – land

1 A: *What's Tom doing in picture 1?*
   B: *He's arriving at the airport and getting off the bus.*

Grammar

Present continuous for future arrangements

Remember and complete.

Positive   **Negative**

Tom's **arriving** next week. Tom .... tomorrow.

Questions

When's Tom ....? On 3rd September.

Are we **meeting** him at the airport?

Yes, we ..../No, we ....

Future time expressions

tomorrow, the day after tomorrow, at the weekend, next week/Tuesday, in three days

Speaking

6 Tomorrow is Saturday. What's Mr Jones doing? Ask and answer.

A: *What's he doing at 10.15?*

B: *He's taking the dog to the vet.*

🔋 UK 🛜   ▶ ✳ 🔋
Saturday

10.15	take dog to the vet
12.30	meet Dylan at McDonald's
3.00	watch the Cambridge United versus Newport match
5.30	collect Tara from choir practice
7.30	have dinner with the Smiths at Browns Restaurant

Grammar

Present simple for fixed timetables

Remember and complete.

What time .... the train **leave**?

The train .... at 14.03 (fourteen oh three).

7 Read the travel information and complete the questions and answers.

Dep.	From	To	Arr.	Dur.
09.15	London Kings Cross	Cambridge	10.03	48m

1 What time *does* the train to Cambridge .... (leave)? When .... it arrive?

The train .... (leave) at .... and .... (arrive) at ....

25	Oxford Circus	2 min
86	Stratford Station	7 min

2 When .... the next bus to Oxford Circus .... (arrive)?

The next bus .... (arrive) in ....

Speaking

8 A: You're Tom's friend, Lizzie. B: You're Tom. Ask and answer about Tom's trip to the UK.

A: *When are you leaving for the UK, Tom?*

B: *I'm leaving in two days.*

E-TICKET NO:	678945039
FLIGHT:	BA1540
FROM:	Chicago (O'Hare) IL
TO:	London (Heathrow) UK
DATE:	12th Sept Dep: 20.35 Arr: 10.00

E-TICKET

Lizzie: When / leave / for the UK?

Tom: I / leave / in two days.

Lizzie: How / you / travel?

Tom: By plane / from Chicago O'Hare airport.

Lizzie: What time / your flight / leave?

Tom: It / leave / 20.35.

Lizzie: What time / it / arrive / in London?

Tom: It / arrive / 10.00 in the morning.

9 Student A: go to page 100.
Student B: go to page 104.

> Now turn to Unit 1B in the Activity Book.

C We're going to do lots of things!

Presentation

1 🎧 1/07 **Listen and read. What are the children going to do?**

Tara: Dad's getting the car. Let's wait here.

Tom: Are we going to drive through London?

Dylan: No, we aren't. But we're going to go sightseeing in London at the weekend.

Tom: Awesome!

Dylan: We're going to do lots of things while you're here, Tom!

Tom: Like what?

Tara: Well, there's a great outdoor centre near us. You can do things like kayaking and other water sports.

Dylan: Or things like mountain biking and climbing.

Tom: Wow! Can you do orienteering – you know, finding places with a map and a compass? It's my favourite.

Dylan We can see. We're going to take you there tomorrow.

Tara: Anyway, I hope you're hungry. You're going to have your first British meal when we get home.

Tom: What's that?

Dylan: Mum's making fish and chips!

2 🎧 1/08 **Listen and repeat the dialogue.**

> **English today**
>
> • You can do things like (kayaking).
> • You know ...

Comprehension

3 **Read again and complete the sentences.**

1 _Mr Jones_ is getting the car.
2 They're going to visit London ....
3 Dylan and Tara are planning to do .... while Tom's in the UK.
4 They're going to take Tom to the .... tomorrow.
5 You can do .... there, like kayaking.
6 They're going to eat .... when they get home.

> **Lesson aims:**
> • talk about free time and after-school activities
> • talk about future plans

Vocabulary: Free time activities

4 🎧 1/09 **Listen and repeat. Label the activities *Indoor (I)*, *Outdoor (O)* or both (I + O).**

do	a (cookery) course *I*
	drama
	judo/karate
	mountain biking *O*
	orienteering
	photography *I + O*
	water sports
go	camping
	dancing
	kayaking
	sightseeing
go to	the cinema
	the park
join	a chess/drama/reading club/the choir
play	chess/computer games
	an instrument (the guitar)
	sports (basketball, rugby, volleyball)
sign up for a (climbing) course	
sing (in a choir)	

5 Look at the pictures. What are their favourite activities?

1 A: *Dylan likes doing photography. He also likes ...*
2 B: *Fran ...*

1 Dylan
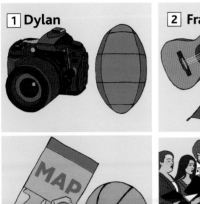

2 Fran

3 Tom
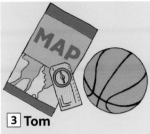

4 Tara

Grammar

going to for future plans

Remember and complete.

Positive
We**'re going to** do lots of things while you're here.

Negative
We .... drive through London.

Questions
.... we .... drive through London?
Yes, we ..../No, we ....
What .... you .... do tomorrow?

6 What plans have Dylan and Tara got for Tom's visit? Look at their list. Ask and answer.

A: *Are they going to go camping in the Lake District?*
B: *Yes, they are.*
A: *Are they going to buy season tickets ... ?*
B: *They're not sure.*

Plans for Tom's trip

go camping in the Lake District ✓
buy season tickets for Cambridge Rugby club ?
go sightseeing in London ✓
spend a week in London ✗
visit Chessington World of Adventures ✓
do a kayaking course at the outdoor centre ?
join the chess club at school ✗

Listening

7 🕐 1/10 Dylan and Fran are deciding what after-school activities they want to do this year. Listen and choose the correct answers.

1 Dylan's going to do _____ this year.
  a a cookery course **(b)** photography **c** drama
2 Fran's going to enter a _____ competition on TV.
  a drama **b** singing **c** cookery
3 _____'s going to join the school choir.
  a Fran **b** Dylan **c** Tom
4 Miss Barnes is _____.
  a a drama student **b** the drama teacher
  c the choir teacher
5 Basketball is _____ in the UK.
  a not very popular **b** very popular
  c everyone's favourite sport
6 Dylan's going to be in the _____ team this year.
  a school rugby **b** UK rugby **c** school football

Speaking

8 You're starting a new school with lots of after-school activities. Look at the information and tick (✓) the activities you want to do. Then ask and answer.

A: *What after-school activities are you going to do this year?*
B: *I'm going to ... . I'm also going to ... . What about you?*

After-school activities

Please find a selection of activities that we offer.
art, chess club, choir, cookery, dance club, drama, film club, karate, learn to play an instrument, photography, reading club, football, basketball, rugby

Writing

9 Read the email from your cousin and write a reply.

Hi!
I'm not sure yet what after-school activities I'm going to do this year. What about you and your friends? What are you going to do? Maybe your ideas can help!
Cheers,
...

> Now turn to Unit 1C in the Activity Book.

Speaking: Buy a train ticket

1   **Listen and read.** *Tom, Dylan and Mr Jones are taking the train to London.*

Dylan: Can we have three return tickets to London King's Cross, please? One adult and two children.

Woman: Cambridge to London King's Cross. Are you returning today?

Dad: Yes, we are.

Woman: Have you got a Railcard? It's cheaper with a Railcard.

Dad: Oh yes. Here you are.

Woman: OK, that's £23.90, please. Are you paying by credit card?

Dad: Yes, just a moment.

Woman: Thank you, remove your card, please.

Dylan: When does the next train leave?

Woman: The next train is at 9.40. It's a fast train.

Tom: Thanks.

Dylan: Dad, what platform does the train to London leave from?

Dad: Let's see ... platform 4. It leaves in three minutes.

Dylan: Ah no! We're going to miss the train.

Dad: Quick boys, run! We can catch it.

2 **Put the dialogue in the correct order. Then listen and check.**

1	**Mum:**	Can I have two return tickets to Birmingham, please? One adult and one child.
	Man:	Thank you. Here's your change.
	Mum:	No, I'm afraid I haven't.
	Man:	Platform 3.
	Mum:	Here you are.
	Man:	The next train is at 11.10.
	Mum:	No, we're returning on Sunday.
	Man:	London to Birmingham. Are you returning today?
	Mum:	Thanks. When does the next train leave?
	Man:	Have you got a Railcard?
	Mum:	What platform does it leave from?
	Man:	Oh, it's cheaper with a Railcard. That's £55.10, please.

English today

- Can I have a single/return ticket to (London)?
- Have you got a Railcard? • Here's your change.
- When does the next train leave?
- The next train is at (9.40).
- What platform does it leave from?

Your turn

3 **Imagine you and your grandma are going to Oxford for the day. Use the information below to help you write a dialogue. Then act it out.**

A: *Can I have two return tickets to Oxford, please? One adult and one child.*

B: *OK. Have you got a Railcard?*

Dep.	From	To	Arr.	Dur.	Return
10.06	London Paddington	Oxford	11.04	58m	£19.90*

* based on 1 adult, 1 child and Railcard

Writing: Describe travel plans

4 Read the email and answer the questions.

send   save

Subject: Saturday in London

Hi Keira,

How are you? My cousin from Canada is staying with us at the moment. We're going to London on Saturday to do some sightseeing. Would you like to meet us?

We're going to visit Buckingham Palace and then we're going to take a riverboat to Greenwich. I'm doing a project about ships at school at the moment so I want to go to the National Maritime Museum.

We're catching the 9.35 train. I'm not sure what time it arrives in London. I can text you when I'm on the train.

I'm looking forward to seeing you on Saturday.

Ronnie

1 When are they going to London?
2 What are they going to do in London?
3 What project is Ronnie doing at school at the moment?
4 What train are they catching?

Writing tip

Check your tenses.

Read your work and make sure you use your tenses correctly.

We use the present simple for ...
– habits and routines.
– fixed timetables in the future.

We use the present continuous for ...
– things happening now.
– future arrangements.

We use *going to* for future plans.

Look at the email in Exercise 4 and find five sentences using a present tense and one sentence using a future tense.

5 Read the email and choose the correct words.

send   save

Subject: Re: Saturday in London

Hi Ronnie,

What a shame! I ¹ *'m not be* / *'m not going to be* in London this Saturday. Dad ² *'s taking* / *takes* us to Longleat Safari Park and then we ³ *'re going to visit* / *visit* Stonehenge. I'm ⁴ *do* / *doing* a History project about it at the moment so I really want to go. But don't forget – we ⁵ *'re coming* / *come* to Cambridge on 25th February!
See you then!

Keira

Your turn

6 Imagine you're planning a family trip to London. Use the information below to write an email to a friend. Invite him/her and tell him/her your plans. Use Exercise 4 to help.

... go to London / Sunday / sightseeing
... visit Madame Tussaud's Waxworks Museum
... go to Sherlock Holmes' house
... ride on the London Eye
... catch the 10.15 train

> Now turn to page 13 in the Activity Book.

Getting around in the UK and the USA

London

People in London use their bikes a lot. Bikes are eco-friendly and also good exercise.

But in London, people usually take public transport for long distances, not their cars or their bikes. Fortunately, London has got a great underground train system. British people call it 'the Tube' and it's their favourite means of transport around London. 'The Tube' is the oldest underground system in the world. The first Tube line opened in 1863. It's very easy to use, it's fast and it can take you all around the city.

The London Underground ('the Tube')

- There are **11** lines and about **270** stations.
- Today more than **3** million people travel by Tube every day.
- Only around **45 percent** of the London Underground is actually under the ground.

San Francisco

In San Francisco people use buses, trains, ferries, streetcars (they're similar to buses but they run on electricity) and cable cars.

Cable cars look really beautiful! They are a piece of San Francisco's history and they first appeared in 1873. The amazing thing about cable cars is that they haven't got an engine. The cars run on rails. Inside the rails there's a cable. This cable moves all the time at a steady speed. The cable pulls the cable car up and down hills and along the streets!

San Francisco cable cars

- Cable cars weigh between **7** and **7.6** tons.
- They run at a steady speed of **14.5 km/ph**.
- There are **three** cable car lines.

New words

appear cable distances eco-friendly
electricity engine ferry line pull along
to run on speed steady system

1 🔊 1/13 **Listen and read. Find these numbers in the text. What do they refer to?**

1 270 *the number of Tube stations in the London Underground*
2 11   4 1873
3 3 million 5 1863

Comprehension

2 **Read again and answer.**
1 What's people's favourite form of transport around London?
2 How old is the London Underground system?
3 Is all of 'the Tube' underground?
4 What's a streetcar?
5 How old is the cable car system in San Francisco?
6 What makes a cable car move?

Listening

3 🔊 1/14 **Diana, Matt and Kelly are presenting their class project. Listen and match the captions (1–3) with the photos (A–C).**
1 The Staten Island Ferry ☐
2 The Greyhound ☐
3 Route 66 ☐

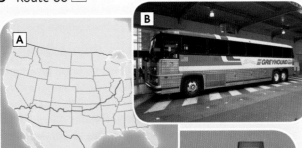

4 🔊 1/15 **Listen again and match the sentences with the photos from Exercise 3.**
1 It travels all over North America [B]
2 You don't have to pay for it. ☐
3 It is a very famous road. ☐
4 It's got a picture of a dog on it. ☐
5 It first opened in 1926. ☐
6 It carries 20 million people a year. ☐

Think about it

How important is public transport where you live? Explain your answers.

Speaking

5 **Ask and answer about getting around your city/town. Use the ideas below.**
A: *What means of public transport are there in ... ?*
B: *There are buses ...*
A: *Do people ... ?*
• means of public transport in this city/town
• whether people use cars
• people's favourite type of public transport
• why they like this (e.g. fast, easy, cheap)

Project: Transport in my city/town

6 **Write about the means of public transport in your city/town. Answer these questions in your text.**
1 What means of public transport are there?
2 Do many people use cars and bikes?
3 Which means of public transport is your favourite?
4 When did it start?
5 How many people use it?
6 Does it have a name?
7 Why do people use it?

Transport in Madrid
People in Madrid use buses, taxis and the Underground. A lot of people use cars but not very many use bikes ... .

F Revision

1 **Unscramble the words and complete the sentences.**

1 My big sister always tells me what to do. She's very
  bossy (ysbos).
2 My brother helps me with my Maths homework and
  knows all the answers. He's very .... (ervlce).
3 My grandad and grandma gave me a bike for my
  birthday. They're very .... (uregneso).
4 My cat sleeps all the time. It's very .... (yzal).
5 My dad goes to work early in the morning and comes
  home at eight o'clock in the evening. He's very
  .... (drah-gwrkoin).
6 You mustn't talk when your teacher is talking. It's
  very .... (duer).
7 My best friend is very good at Art. Her pictures are
  always the best. She's very .... (evitacre).
8 I always want to do things quickly. I'm not very
  .... (tipatne).

2 **Complete the chat. Use the present simple or present continuous. Then act it out.**

SARA: Hey, Dylan, ¹ _is Tom staying_ (Tom/stay) with you now? What's he like?

DYLAN: He's cool, very cheerful. But he ² .... (not play) rugby.

SARA: Well, kids ³ .... (not usually play) rugby in the USA. ⁴ .... (he/play) basketball?

DYLAN: Yes, he's brilliant. He ⁵ .... (teach) me to play at the moment. Well, not now, right now he ⁶ .... (sleep).

SARA: Really? Why?

DYLAN: He ⁷ .... (often fall) asleep at this time. It's night time in the USA!

3 **Lisa is going on an exchange trip to Chicago. Put her travel notes in the correct order.**

Trip to Chicago:

☐ *11.00 get on the plane*
☐ *8.20 check in my luggage (32 kilos only)*
1 *8.00 arrive at London Heathrow Airport*
☐ *11.20 take off (flight time 7 hours and 55 minutes)*
☐ *10.00 go through security*
☐ *15.00 meet Milton family*
☐ *14.15 land O'Hare International Airport (five-hour time difference)*

4 **Complete the email with the words in the box.**

doesn't   going   're   leave   meeting   ~~arriving~~

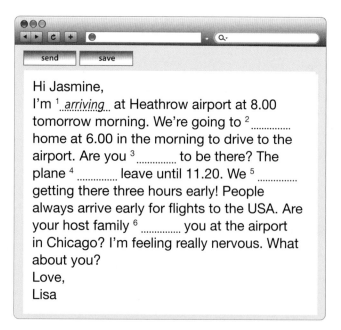

Hi Jasmine,
I'm ¹ _arriving_ at Heathrow airport at 8.00 tomorrow morning. We're going to ² .... home at 6.00 in the morning to drive to the airport. Are you ³ .... to be there? The plane ⁴ .... leave until 11.20. We ⁵ .... getting there three hours early! People always arrive early for flights to the USA. Are your host family ⁶ .... you at the airport in Chicago? I'm feeling really nervous. What about you?
Love,
Lisa

5 **Ask and answer about Lisa's trip.**

A: *What time is Lisa arriving at Heathrow airport?*
B: *She's arriving at eight o'clock in the morning.*

6 Look at the pictures. What after-school activities are they going to do this year? Ask and answer.

1 **A:** *What's he going to do?*
   B: *He's going to do photography and he's going to … . He isn't going to do karate.*

1

2

3

7 Complete the dialogue with phrases a–f. Then act it out.

Fran: Can I have [1] *two return tickets* to Leeds, please? One adult and one child.
Woman: London to Leeds. Sure. Have you got [2] .... ?
Fran: Yes, we have. Just a minute.
Woman: Thank you. And when [3] .... ?
Fran: Next Saturday.
Woman: Saturday 25th. OK. [4] ....
Fran: Here you are. When does [5] .... ?
Woman: The next train is at 10.15.
Fran: [6] .... it leave from?
Woman: Platform 4.
Fran: Thanks.

a the next train leave
b What platform does
c ~~two return tickets~~
d a Railcard
e That's £82.45, please.
f are you returning

8 Read the email in Exercise 4 again. Find an example of each of these tenses.

1 present continuous for future arrangements
   We're getting there three hours early!
2 present simple for fixed timetables
3 *going to* for future plans
4 present continuous for something happening now
5 present simple for habits and routines

Pronunciation: falling intonation in *wh-* questions

9 🔊 1/16 Listen and repeat.

Who's your favourite singer?
Do you like TV?
What's your favourite hobby?
Do you like me?

10 🔊 1/17 Listen to the questions. Draw arrows to show rising ⤴ or falling ⤵ intonation.

1 Do you like watching TV? ⤴
2 What are your favourite programmes?
3 When do you watch TV?
4 Do you have a TV in your bedroom?
5 What do you do in your free time?

My progress

11 Read and tick (✓).

I can:	
talk about appearance and personality. *I've got dark curly hair. I'm very polite.*	☐
talk about routines. *Mum never works at weekends.*	☐
talk about things happening now. *My brother isn't living at home at the moment.*	☐
talk about transport and travel. *Our train leaves at 9.00 (in the morning).*	☐
talk about future arrangements. *Tom is arriving on 3rd September.*	☐
talk about free time and after-school activities. *I like doing photography.*	☐
talk about future plans. *I'm going to join the choir.*	☐
buy a train ticket. *Can I have two return tickets to London, please?*	☐

> Turn to Unit 1 Check in the Activity Book on page 14.

2 Technology and you

A The teachers will be robots.

Lesson aim:
· make predictions about the future of technology

Presentation

1 Read the predictions in the chart. Then read predictions A–F below. Think about these questions and complete the chart.

· When will predictions A–F come true?
· Are they likely to happen or unlikely to happen?

Comprehension

2 1/18 Listen and check your answers.

TOMORROW'S WORLD: What will life be like in the future?

MOST LIKELY			LESS LIKELY
Smart TVs will be connected to the Internet.	1 ......E......	in one or two years' time	People will use eco-friendly electric bikes to get around town.
Every home will have wireless Internet (wi-fi).	All students will have tablet computers in the classroom.	in five years' time	2 ....
3	All classrooms will be connected to the Internet.	in ten years' time	Solar-powered clothes will charge your mobile phone and MP3 player.
Planes won't need pilots. They will fly by remote control. 4	You won't go to school to learn. Students will study online at home.	in twenty-five years' time	People won't travel to other places on holiday. They will have virtual holidays. 5 .... We will log on to the Internet directly from our brain.
Many buildings will be higher than 10 kilometres.	6	in fifty years' time	Superhumans will buy bionic arms and legs made of metal and plastic.

A Bionic eyes will be on sale.

B Cars won't use petrol. They will have solar panels on the roof and use solar energy.

C People will choose their children's personality.

D Smart homes will cook the food, clean the floor and repair themselves.

E Smartphones will be super-thin and bendy.

F Household robots will bring you dinner as you watch TV.

Key
- Home life
- Education
- Transport and travel
- Other technologies

Vocabulary: Technology

3 🔊 **1/19** Listen and repeat. Circle the things that you/your family have.

> app   (mobile phone) charger   digital camera
> electric bike   games console   laptop
> (TV) remote control   robot
> (bendy) smartphone   solar panels
> tablet computer   virtual (games)   wi-fi

4 Which of the things in Exercise 3 ...

1 didn't exist five years ago/ten years ago?
2 can you carry in your school bag?
3 are the most useful on holiday?
4 would you like to have?
5 will change the most in the future?

Grammar

Future predictions with *will/won't*

Positive
People **will use** eco-friendly electric bikes to get around town.
Planes **will be** able to fly without pilots.

Negative
Planes **won't need** pilots.
Students **won't go** to school to learn.

Questions
What will life **be** like in fifty years' time?
Will homes **be** different?
Yes, they **will**./No, they **won't**.
won't = will not
The future form of *can* = *will/won't be able to*

5 Read the text in Exercise 1 again and answer the questions.

1 How will education be different in ten years' time? in twenty-five years' time?
  In ten years' time, all classrooms will be connected to the Internet.
2 How will buildings change in the future?
3 How will home life be different in the future?
4 How will transport be different in the future?
5 What will people do in fifty years' time?

Listening

6 🔊 **1/20** Listen to each conversation and tick (✓) the correct picture.

1 What's Dad looking for?

 A ☐ 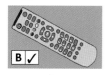 B ✓  C ☐

2 What's Tara listening to music on?

 A ☐  B ☐  C ☐

3 What year is the article about?

 A ☐   B ☐   C ☐

4 What's Dylan looking at?

 A ☐  B ☐  C ☐

About you

7 What do you think your life will be like in ten years' time? Ask and answer.

1 **A:** *Where will you be in ten years?*
   B: *I won't be in Spain. I'll be in the USA!*

1 Where / be?
2 What job / have?
3 Have / family?
4 Have / car?
5 What / your home / be like?
6 What kind of holidays / you / have?

Writing

8 Write your predictions about life in seventy years' time.

• What will people be like?
• What will homes be like?
• What will young people do in their free time?

> **Life in seventy years' time**
>
> People will have bionic eyes and metal arms and legs. Their clothes will have ... . Homes will ... .

> Now turn to Unit 2A in the Activity Book.

B If you click on this, ...

Lesson aims:
· explain how to use technical devices
· talk about hypothetical future situations

Presentation

1 🔘(1/21) **Listen and read. Choose the correct words.**

Grandma: Fran, can you help me? I want to send
¹ *a letter* / *an email* to your uncle in Italy but I don't know how to use your mum's laptop.

Fran: Sure, Grandma. Let me see. OK, you're in Mum's inbox. If you click on this button, a 'new message' box will come up.

Grandma: Oh, I see. So I type into that.

Fran: Right. Then you'll need to add Uncle Marcello's ² *address* / *name*.

Grandma: Well, I think it's Via Venezia but I don't ³ *know* / *remember* the number. Can you pass me my address book? If you open my bag, you'll see it.

Fran: Er, Grandma, you need his email address, not his home address.

Grandma: Oh, silly me! ⁴ *I don't think* / *I'm not sure* I've got that.

Fran: If we look in Mum's contacts list, we'll probably find it. Yes, here it is.

Grandma: Thanks, Fran. Don't go away. I won't be able to remember what to do!

Fran: No problem, Grandma. By the way, ⁵ *I'm afraid* / *I'm sorry* you won't be able to print your email. Our printer's broken.

2 🔘(1/22) **Listen and repeat the dialogue.**

> **English today**
> · Can you help me?   · By the way, ...
> · Silly me!   · I'm afraid ...

Comprehension

3 **Read again and complete the sentences with one word from the dialogue.**

1 Fran's uncle lives in __Italy__.
2 Grandma wants to send him a/an ....
3 Grandma is using Fran's mum's ....
4 Grandma hasn't got Uncle Marcello's email ....
5 Fran's mum has got it in her .... list.
6 The .... isn't working.

Vocabulary: Using technology

4 🔘(1/23) **Listen and repeat. Then match nine nouns from the box with the objects in the picture.**

> **Nouns:** battery   contacts (list)   e-book reader   email address   icon   keyboard   mouse   online game   plug   printer   screen   transformer   USB cable   website
>
> **Verbs:** click (on)   delete   download   log on   plug in/unplug   print   save   send (emails, photographs)   shut down   surf the Internet   switch off/on

1 *plug*

5 Match six verbs from the box in Exercise 4 with the icons.

1 *delete*

 1   2   3   4   5   6

Grammar

First conditional + *will/won't*

Positive

If you **open** my bag, you**'ll see** my address book.
If we **look in** Mum's contacts list, we**'ll find** Uncle's address.

Negative

If you **go away**, I **won't be able to** remember what to do.

Questions

What **will happen** if I click on this button? The computer **will shut down**.
If I **unplug** the computer, **will** it **shut down**?
No, it **won't**. It**'ll run** on battery.

Choose the correct tense.

We use the *present simple / future* in the *if* clause.

Speaking

6 Ask and answer. Use the future form.

1 **A:** *Why is it important to save my work?*
   B: *If your computer crashes, you'll lose any unsaved work.*

1 Why is it important to save my work?
   If your computer crashes, you / lose / any unsaved work.

2 How do I print my work?
   If you click on the PRINT icon, the computer / download / your work / to printer.

3 Why is it important to switch my computer off?
   If you switch it off and unplug the transformer, you / save / electricity.

4 How do I download my photos from my camera?
   If you want to download your photos, you / need / a USB cable.

5 How do I read e-books on my mobile phone?
   If you want to read e-books on your phone, you / have to download / the right app.

7 What will happen if there's a power cut? Complete the sentences with the correct forms of the verbs.

1 If there __'s__ (be) a power cut, we __won't have__ (not have) any electricity.

2 If we .... (not have) any electricity, our computers .... (not work).

3 If our computers .... (not work), we .... (not be able to) go on the Internet.

4 If we .... (not can) go on the Internet, we .... (not be able to) email our friends.

5 If we .... (not can) email our friends, we .... (have to) text them on our phones.

6 If our batteries .... (run out), we .... (not be able to) charge them!

7 If we .... (not can) recharge our phones, we .... (have to) go out and meet our friends.

8 If we .... (go out) and meet our friends, we .... (have) fun!

8 Student A: go to page 100.
   Student B: go to page 104.

Writing

9 Complete the sentences. Use Exercise 7 or your own ideas. Then write your own sentence.

1 If I don't have to go to school to learn, ...
2 If robots become as intelligent as people, ...
3 If people live on Mars, ...
4 If ... .

> Now turn to Unit 2B in the Activity Book.

Speaking: Offer help and make decisions

1   **Listen and read.** *Tara's got a new digital camera. She's asking Dylan for help.*

1

Tara: Hey, Dylan, how do I download photos from my new camera?

Dylan: I'll show you. First, you need a USB cable.

Tara: OK. I think it's in the camera box. Shall I go and get it?

Dylan: Yes, please. I can't use the one from my camera. They're different.

2

Tara: OK, the camera is connected to the computer. Now what do I do?

Dylan: If you click on the camera icon, the computer will start downloading the photos.

Tara: OK. Hmm, am I doing it right? Nothing's happening.

Dylan: That's strange. Let me have a look.

3

Tara: All right. You sit here, then.

Dylan: Something's wrong. It's still not working.

Tara: Look, I'll just ask Tom to help me. He's good with computers.

Dylan: No, I'll do it. Here. Oops!

Tara: Oh, Dylan, no! Now the computer's crashing!

2 1/25 **Complete the dialogue with sentences a–e. Then listen and check.**

Fran: Tom, how do I download music from the computer to my MP3 player?

Tom: [1] *I'll show you*. First, you need a USB cable to connect the MP3 player to the computer.

Fran: I've got one in my room. [2] ....

Tom: No, don't worry. [3] .... They're the same. OK, now, if you click on the MP3 icon, it'll start downloading the music.

Fran: Am I doing it right? Nothing's happening.

Tom: That's strange. Let me have a look.

Fran: [4] .... She's got the same MP3 player.

Tom: [5] .... There you are, it's downloading.

Fran: Thanks, Tom!

a I'll use mine.	**d** No, I'll do it.
b I'll ask Mum to help me.	**e** Shall I go and get it?
c ~~I'll show you.~~	

English today

- I'll show you (how to do it).
- Shall I go and get it?
- Let me have a look.
- I'll ask (Tom) to help me.
- I'll do/fix it.

Your turn

3 **Use the ideas below and Exercise 2 to help you write a dialogue. Then act it out.**

A: Ask how to download a video from your phone to your computer.

B: Offer to show Student A. Say you need a USB cable.

A: Your mum's got a USB cable. Offer to get it.

B: Say you've got a USB cable. Say, if you click on the phone icon on the computer, it'll download the video.

A: Say nothing is happening. Your cousin Alison knows a lot about downloading videos.

B: Say you'll do it.

Writing: Offer to help

4 Read the emails and complete the sentences.

Subject: digital camera   send   save

Hi Georgia,

Help! 😞 I'm having problems with my digital camera. Yesterday, I asked Dad to help me download photos from it. We downloaded the photos but now I can't switch the camera on again! I really need to take some more photos for my school project. Can you help me or do I have to take it back to the shop?

Love,

Jenny

Subject: Re: digital camera

Hi Jenny,

This sounds serious. I don't think I can help you but my friend Alice is brilliant with technology. I'll ask her to come over this afternoon. If you bring your camera to my house, she'll look at it. I'm sure she won't mind. She loves fixing things! If she can't help, I'll lend you my camera. It's a bit old but it takes good photos. You can use it for your school project.

Bye for now,

Georgia

---

1 _Jenny's_ camera isn't working.
2 .... can't help her.
3 .... will look at Jenny's camera.
4 .... will give Jenny her old camera.

Writing tip

Apostrophes (')

We use an apostrophe ...

– to show that some letters are missing.

I've got = I have got   they won't = they will not
John's here = John is here

– to make the possessive form of a word.

the boy's name   John's bike.

Note: *It's = It is   **It's** Monday today.*
*Its = possessive   The dog wagged **its** tail.*

Look at Georgia's email in Exercise 4 and circle all the shortened words. Then read it aloud, saying the words in full.

---

5 Read the texts and add the missing apostrophes. There are ten missing apostrophes.

News > Technology
Technology blog

It's finally here! If youre into technology, youll want to get this new bendable phone the minute its in your local shop!

Robodog will look after your home when youre out. It looks like a dangerous dog. Its one metre long and weighs 40 kilograms. Its battery will last about four hours. It costs £10,000 so it isnt cheap!

Ill be back home at 4 o'clock. I havent got keys so please dont go out. Mum

---

Your turn

6 Read the email from your friend Edgar and write a reply. Use Exercise 4 to help.

• offer to help
• say where and when to meet
• offer to lend him your MP3 player if you can't fix his

Subject: MP3 player   send   save

Hi,

Help! I've got a problem with my MP3 player. I can't switch it on! I really need to download some dance music to play at the party on Saturday. Can you help me?

Cheers,

Edgar

Subject: Re: MP3 player

Hi Edgar,

Don't worry. I think I can help.

> Now turn to page 23 in the Activity Book.

IT and the classroom

How can technology help students learn? Will learning change?

1

A school in Japan is using a robot in the classroom to teach Science and Technology. The robot can look happy, sad or angry and is just like a human. In some schools in Japan – for example, in the countryside – there aren't enough teachers to teach Science and Technology lessons. So this remote-controlled robot is a great idea. It's amazing that scientists can now programme a robot to replace a human teacher. Maybe in the future, *all* schools will use robot teachers!

Josué, 13, Brazil

2

If every student in the class has a tablet computer and our school has a wi-fi network, learning will be much more interesting. We'll be able to work together and do projects and share ideas. We'll be able to work at our own speed when our teacher gives us exercises. Also, we'll be able to connect with students in classrooms all over the world and talk to each other live online. It's a great way to improve our English!

Marta, 14, Spain

3

Interactive video games are lots of fun and they're also educational. Games can teach students about the real world. Some games teach us about different places and different times in history. One day maybe we won't need books to learn about history. We'll use special headsets or glasses and go into a virtual environment. We'll experience what life was really like.

Tosia, 13, Poland

New words

at (our) own speed   connect (with)   educational
experience (*v*)   headset   improve   interactive
programme (*v*)   (talk) live (online)   real   share
time(s) (in history)   virtual environment

Reading

1 **1 26** **Listen and read. Match the headings (a–c) with the texts (1–3).**

a   Classrooms without walls .....

b   Play and learn .....

c   No more teachers .....

Comprehension

2 Read again and choose the correct answers. There are two for each question.

1 With robot teachers ...
   a everyone can stay at home and learn.
   (b) all schools can teach Science and Technology.
   c students won't also need a real teacher.
2 With a school wi-fi network ...
   a you can connect to classrooms around the world.
   b you can buy new computers.
   c you can work at your own speed in class.
3 Interactive video games ...
   a make learning fun.
   b will never replace books.
   c can teach students about subjects like history.

Study tip

You'll remember new words better if you write an example sentence in your vocabulary notebook.

connect

You can connect to the Internet in some cafés.

Now write example sentences for these words.

improve   educational   communicate

Listening

3 Listen and complete the text.

English forum *online*

On today's programme, three students talk about their plans for using ¹ ..*wireless*.. computer networks in their schools.

SCHOOL 1: **Sonia**
Plan: Create a networking site for the school.
How will it help?   Students will be able to ² ....
                     with students in other classes.

SCHOOL 2: **Sebastian**
Plan: Play an online ³ .... with
                     schools in other countries.
How will it help?   Will help students to ⁴ ....
                     their English.

SCHOOL 3: **Petra**
Plan: Start an Internet ⁵ ....
                     station and interview students in English about
                     the kind of music they like.
How will it help?   Students will be able to ⁶ ....
                     their favourite music.

Think about it

What are the advantages of using technology in the classroom? Are there any disadvantages?

Speaking

4 Choose from the list below three items of technology to help students learn English. Discuss in groups and decide which three will be the most useful.

A: *What about a games console? We'll be able to play games and watch films in class!*
B: *I think wi-fi in the classroom is better.*
C: *OK, so let's choose wi-fi in the classroom.*

Item	How will it help?
games console	play games, watch films
tablet computer for every student	easy to carry, email homework to teacher, won't need to share computer at home
school networking site	communicate with students in other classes, share ideas
robot or virtual teacher	students won't be embarrassed, fun
wi-fi in the classroom	connect to the Internet in class, lessons more interactive, work together in class.

Writing: Technology that will help our school

5 Complete the report.

Technology that will help our school

Our group chose these items of technology for learning English.

Our first choice was ¹ .... in every classroom. If we can connect to the Internet in class, we'll be able to work together on projects. Lessons will be more interesting.

Our second choice was ² .... for every student. They're light and easy to use. You don't need a monitor or keyboard. If every student has one, our school bags won't be so heavy.

Our third choice was ³ .... Some games are educational and we'll use it to watch DVDs, too.

6 Write a report about your choices in Exercise 4. Use Exercise 5 to help.

E Revision

1 Match the explanations with the words in the box.

charger	games console	~~smartphone~~
digital camera	robot	remote control
USB cable	headset	tablet solar power

1 You can use this to send text messages to your friends. _smartphone_

2 If you like taking photos, you'll need this. ....

3 You can use this to play video games. ....

4 You can use this to switch on the TV from the sofa. ....

5 If you want to download photos to your computer, you'll need this. ....

6 If every student has one of these, they won't need to share the home computer. ....

7 Some cars will use this in the future to replace petrol. ....

8 If you have a mobile phone, you'll need one of these to charge the battery. ....

9 If you don't want to do household jobs, you'll need one of these. ....

10 You'll need this if you want to play virtual reality games in the future. ....

2 **What will life be like in seventy years? Write the questions in your notebook. Then write your answers.**

Education

1 be real teachers / virtual teachers?

Will there be real teachers or virtual teachers?

There won't be real teachers. There will only be virtual teachers.

2 students learn in classrooms / online at home?

Transport and travel

3 people go away on holiday / have virtual holidays?

Home life

4 people do housework / robots do everything?

Free time

5 people meet friends in real life / only talk online?

3 Label the icons with the words in the box.

app	contacts list	delete	download	inbox
~~Internet~~	print	save	wi-fi	

1 _Internet_ **2** .... **3** .... **4** .... **5** ....

6 .... **7** .... **8** .... **9** ....

4 **Complete the dialogues. Use a word or phrase from A and B and the future form.**

A	B
~~bring your mobile phone~~	download it
switch it on	find it
like it	do it
get the right mobile phone app	~~show you how~~
click on the printer icon	~~to use it~~
you add it to your contacts list	work
	help

Dialogue 1

Gran: I've got a mobile phone at home but I don't know how to use it.

You: If you _bring your mobile phone_ with you next time, I _'ll show you how to use it_.

Dialogue 2

Dad: Can I read an e-book on my mobile?

You: Yes, you can. If you ...., it .... you download e-books.

Dialogue 3

A friend: My camera isn't working!

You: That's because it's off. If you ...., it ....

Dialogue 4

Mum: That's a nice song!

You: If you ...., I .... for you.

Dialogue 5

Grandad: I'll write your email address in my address book.

You: No, Grandad. If ...., you .... more easily.

Dialogue 6

Your cousin: How can I print my homework?

You: If you ...., the computer .... automatically.

5 Complete the dialogue with sentences a–h. Then act it out.

You: ¹ *How do I download video from my video camera to my laptop?*

Your friend: I'll show you. First you need a USB cable.

You: ² ....

Your friend: ³ ....

You: OK, now what do I do?

Your friend: ⁴ ....

You: ⁵ ....

Your friend: ⁶ ....

You: All right. Thanks.

Your friend: That can't be right. It's still not working.

You: ⁷ ....

Your friend: ⁸ ....

You: Thanks!

---

a That's strange. Let me have a look.

b I've got one in my room. Shall I go and get it?

c How do I download video from my video camera to my laptop?

d No, don't worry. I'll use this one here. They're the same.

e If you click on the video camera icon, it will download the video.

f No, I'll fix it. Here. It's ready.

g Hmm … Am I doing it right? Nothing's happening.

h I'll ask my cousin, George. He's good at fixing things.

---

6 Read the emails. Complete the second email with the verbs in the box. Use the present simple or future form.

---

ask   have   lend   bring   not mind

Subject: laptop

send   save

Hi Vicky,

Help! 🙁 I'm having problems with my laptop. I switch it on and it works for half an hour. Then it suddenly shuts down and stops working. I really need it for my school project. Can you help or do I need to take it back to the shop?

Bye for now,
Chris

Subject: Re: laptop

Hi Chris,

This sounds serious. I can't help you but my friend, Peter, is brilliant with computers.¹ *I'll ask* him to come over this afternoon.
If you ² .... your laptop to my house, he ³ .... a look at it.
I'm sure he ⁴ ...., he loves fixing things! If he can't fix it,
I ⁵ .... you my old laptop.

Talk later,
Vicky

Pronunciation: /aɪ/, /aɪl/

7 🔵 1/28 Listen and repeat.

Thanks, **I** got your email.
I'll write one back to you.
I'll send you lots of photos
From m**y** holiday in Peru.

8 🔵 1/29 Choose the correct words. Then listen and check.

1 *I* / I'll eat an apple every day.
2 I / I'll download this song for you.
3 I / I'll come to your party.
4 I / I'll know his email address.
5 Oh no! I / I'll miss the bus!
6 I / I'll play volleyball on Saturdays.

My progress

9 Read and tick (✓).

I can:	
make predictions about the future of technology. *Cars won't use petrol. Smart TVs will be connected to the Internet.*	☐
explain how to use technical devices. *You need to add Uncle Marcello's address.*	☐
talk about hypothetical future situations. *If you don't save your work, you'll lose it.*	☐
offer help and make decisions. *I'll show you how to do it. Shall I go and get the USB cable?*	☐

> Turn to Unit 2 Check in the Activity Book on page 24.

pick and mix

Fun Time!

Read the riddles about famous film and TV characters and guess who they are. Can you write a riddle about your favourite film or TV character?

Who am I?

1

I fly through the air but I haven't got wings.
I wear a metal suit and fight evil things.
I'm clever and love to have money and fame.
I'm Tony Stark but I've got another name.
ronI naM

2

Some think I'm pretty, and some do not.
There's a big green man I love a lot.
I'm bossy, I'm kind, I can get angry.
I sometimes eat eggs … when I'm hungry.
ssPcrine naFoi

3

I haven't got a lot of hair,
To tell the truth, I don't care.
I know I'm not clever, I'm selfish and lazy
But I love my Marge, and she loves me.
mreHo nsompSi

JUST JOKING!

Why did the computer get glasses?

To improve its web sight!

What stays in the corner but travels all over the world?

A stamp.

Quick Quiz

Are you a technology whiz? Do the quiz to find out!

1 Laptops and tablets are …
   a websites.
   ⓑ computers.
   c games.

2 WWW stands for …
   a Watch Where you Walk.
   b Wild Wild West.
   c World Wide Web.

3 The first computer mouse was made of …
   a wood.
   b plastic.
   c paper.

4 *Spacewar* was the first …
   a film about the Internet.
   b online album.
   c computer game.

5 Solar energy comes from …
   a the sea.
   b the sun.
   c petrol.

6 The first iPhone came out in …
   a 1960.
   b 1998.
   c 2007.

7 The … invented the first robot hundreds of years ago.
   a Chinese
   b Japanese
   c Americans

8 Bill Gates started the company …
   a Microsoft.
   b Sony.
   c Apple Macintosh.

Guess what?

In 1900, an American engineer called John Elfreth Watkins made some predictions about the year 2000. Read the text. What inventions did he predict?

Predictions by John Elfreth Watkins in 1900

People will be able to send photographs from any distance. In a hundred years, if there is a battle in China, photographs will be in the newspapers one hour later. Wireless telephone and telegraph circuits will go all around the world. A husband in the middle of the Atlantic Ocean will be able to speak to his wife sitting at home in Chicago. We will be able to telephone China just as we telephone New York from Brooklyn.

People will see around the world. Cameras thousands of miles apart will connect to screens at opposite ends and show us all kinds of people and things.

Trains will run two miles a minute normally. Express trains will run one hundred and fifty miles per hour.

THE LADIES' HOME JOURNAL

WHAT MAY HAPPEN IN THE NEXT HUNDRED YEARS
By JOHN ELFRETH WATKINS, JR.

How to ... predict the weather.

Here are four ways to make weather predictions. Do you think they're true? Do you know any more ways to predict the weather?

1 It will probably rain if the grass is dry early in the morning, there are clouds and it's a bit windy. If the grass is a bit wet, it won't rain.

2 Remember this rhyme: 'Red sky at night, shepherd's delight. Red sky in the morning, shepherd's warning.'
If the sky is very red in the west when the sun goes down, it will be hot and sunny.
If the sky is very red in the east when the sun comes up, it will probably rain.

3 Close your eyes and smell the air. If you can smell the flowers, it will probably rain. Flowers smell strong in wet air.

4 Hair goes curly when it's wet. If you've got curly hair and your hair goes even more curly, it will probably rain.

A He used to help in the kitchen.

Lesson aims:
- talk about past events
- talk about things that happened in the past but not now
- talk about abilities in the past

A star chef

Jamie Oliver is a British chef. He's famous for his TV programmes and cookery books. He's also well-known for his campaign for healthy food in British schools. He started cooking years ago when he was a child. Read on to find out more.

Jamie was born in 1975 and grew up in Essex, near London. As a child he didn't mind new and unusual food. He wasn't fussy at all, not like other kids!

Jamie could cook from an early age. When he was eight years old, he used to help in the kitchen of his parents' restaurant. He could only do easy jobs but he enjoyed the work. He used to stand on a chair because he couldn't reach the work surface!

Jamie loved cooking so he decided to become a chef. When he was sixteen, he left school and went to a catering college in London and got a diploma. Because of his talent, hard work and cheerful personality, he became successful. He is now known all around the world and earns a very good living!

Presentation

1 (1/30) Listen and read. What's Jamie famous for?

Comprehension

2 Read again and answer *True* (T) or *False* (F).

1 Jamie thinks school food isn't always healthy. [T]
2 When he was a child, he didn't like unusual food. □
3 His parents have a restaurant. □
4 He didn't like cooking when he was eight years old. □
5 At sixteen, he went to catering college. □
6 He is famous only in the UK. □

Vocabulary: Education and work

3 (1/31) Listen and repeat. Make two lists under the headings *Education* and *Work*.

become famous/ successful	go to college/university
	leave school
do well at school	pass exams
earn a living/money	start school
find/get a job (as a chef)	study hard
get a degree/diploma	work hard

Education	Work
do well at school	*become famous/successful*

4 Number the activities in Exercise 3 in the order they usually happen. Then compare with a partner.

1 start school   2 study hard

Grammar

Past simple

Jamie **started** cooking years **ago**.

He **didn't mind** unusual food as a child.

Did he **leave** school at sixteen?

Yes, he **did**./No, he **didn't**.

Why did he **go** to catering college?

5 Find the past simple form of these verbs in the text in Exercise 1 and write them under the correct heading.

| ~~become~~ | ~~decide~~ | do | enjoy | get | go |
| grow up | leave | love | start | work | |

Regular		Irregular	
Present	Past	Present	Past
decide	decided	become	became

6 Write questions and answers. Then ask and answer with a partner.

1 Where / Jamie Oliver / grow up?
   Where did Jamie Oliver grow up? He grew up in Essex.
2 Why / he / become / a chef?
3 When / he / leave / school?
4 What / he / get / at college?
5 he / work / hard?

Grammar

used to

When he was eight, Jamie **used to help** in his parents' kitchen.

He **didn't use to be** famous. Now he's famous all around the world.

Speaking

7 A: You're Tom. B: You're Tara. Ask and answer.

1 A: *When I was eight, I used to go to school by bus. Now I ride my bike. What about you?*

		Then	Now
1	Tom:	go to school by bus	ride bike
2	Tara:	hate eating fish	like it
3	Tom:	tidy my room once a week	tidy it every day
4	Tara:	like reggae music	can't stand it

Grammar

could

Positive and negative

Jamie **could cook** from an early age.

He **couldn't do** difficult jobs as a child.

Questions

Could he **cook** when he was fifteen?

Yes, he **could**./No, he **couldn't**.

Speaking

8 Make questions. Then ask and answer.

1 A: *Could you cook when you were eight?*
   B: *No, I couldn't.*

1 cook / eight?
2 swim / three?
3 speak English / four?
4 ride a bike / eight?
5 use a computer / six?
6 read / five?

Writing

9 Write a short article about American chef Rachael Ray. Use the information in her profile.

Rachael Ray is an American ... . She's famous for ... . She's also ... . Rachael was born ... and ... . When she was a child, ...

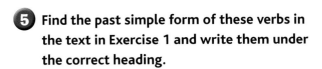

Rachael Ray

Occupation	chef
Famous for	TV cookery series; her charity to help children eat healthier food
Born	1968
Grew up	Massachusetts and New York State, USA
Early life	used to watch mother cooking in family restaurant; could never bake cakes or make coffee but enjoyed cooking
Career	in mid-twenties, used to teach cookery classes; got first TV cookery series in 2001

> Now turn to Unit 3A in the Activity Book.

B We were looking for you!

Lesson aims:
• describe past experiences
• use prepositions of movement

Presentation

1 🔊 1/32 **Listen and read. Choose the correct words.**

Tara, Tom and Dylan are visiting a stately home near London.

Tara: There you are! We were looking for you everywhere!

Tom: I was in the ¹ *bookshop /* (*library.*)

Dylan: The library? What were you doing there?

Tom: I was looking at the ² *books / pictures* when I heard a voice from behind the bookcase.

Tara: A voice?

Tom: Yes, and you'll never believe this! While I was pressing my ear against the bookcase, it suddenly swung ³ *closed / open*.

Tara: No way! A secret door!

Tom: Yes! I fell through the door into a private ⁴ *dining room / restaurant*!

Tara: Really? Then what?

Tom: Well, there was a woman in there in an old-fashioned ⁵ *dress / hat* and a wig.

Dylan: A ghost?!

Tom: No! She was just one of the tour guides! I was in the staff room!

Tara: How embarrassing!

2 🔊 1/33 **Listen and repeat the dialogue.**

> **English today**
> • There you are!
> • Then what?
> • How (embarrassing)!

Comprehension

3 **Read again and complete the summary.**

¹ *Tom* had an embarrassing experience last week. He was in the ² .... at a stately home. He ³ .... a noise so he pressed his ⁴ .... against a bookcase and listened. Suddenly a door opened and he ⁵ .... into a secret room. Inside, he saw a ⁶ .... in an old-fashioned dress and a wig. She wasn't a ⁷ ...., she was a tour ⁸ .... and he was in the staff room!

Vocabulary: Prepositions of movement

4 🔊 1/34 **Listen and repeat. Match the prepositions with the pictures.**

across	along	around	into	out of
over	through	towards	under	

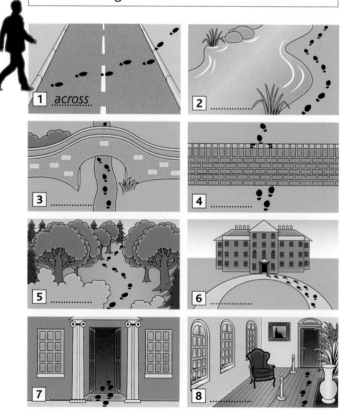

1 *across*
2 ....
3 ....
4 ....
5 ....
6 ....
7 ....
8 ....

5 **Where did the mystery man go? Did he come out of the house?**

First, he went across a road. Then, ...

Grammar

Past continuous

Positive and negative

We **were looking** for you everywhere.

I **wasn't touching** the pictures.

Questions

Were you **standing** in a secret passage?

Yes, I **was**./No, I **wasn't**.

What were you **doing** there?

6 **What you were doing at these times? Ask and answer.**

1 **A:** *What were you doing at nine o'clock last night?*
   B: *I was watching TV. What were you doing?*

1 nine o'clock last night
2 seven o'clock this morning
3 five o'clock last Saturday
4 six o'clock last Wednesday

Grammar

Past continuous with *when* and *while*

I was looking at the books **when** I <u>heard</u> a voice.

While I <u>was looking</u> at the books, I heard a voice.

Listening

7 **🎵 1/35 Listen to the radio programme and choose the correct answers.**

The boy on the radio show …
  Ⓐ was visiting Los Angeles.
  b was watching a film about Los Angeles.

2 Daniel and his family …
  a were having lunch in a diner.
  b were looking for a bank.

3 While they were sitting in the diner, …
  a Daniel's mum went to the bank across the road.
  b they saw a bank robbery outside.

4 A man was coming out of the bank when …
  a a woman shouted 'Stop him!'
  b a police officer stopped him.

5 The man was running away when …
  a the woman knocked him over.
  b a cyclist knocked him over.

6 A camera crew on the back of a truck …
  a was recording the news.
  b was filming the actors.

8 **Write sentences about what Daniel saw. Use *when* and *while*. Then retell the story to your partner.**

Daniel and his parents were visiting family in LA. While they were having lunch in a diner, … .

Writing

9 **Look at the pictures. Write sentences with *when* and *while*. Use the prompts to help.**

1 *While Sally and her family were having a picnic in the park, a boy … .*

1 Sally and family / picnic // boy / fall into / river

2 boy / shout for help // man / jump in / to save

3 man and boy / stand / on riverbank // camera crew / arrive

4 camera crew / film / actors // Sally and family / see / them

> **Now turn to Unit 3B in the Activity Book.**

C No one believed us!

Lesson aims:
• describe objects
• use indefinite pronouns

Presentation

1 **36** Listen and read. Match the photos and headlines with the news stories.

Strange but true!

1 ....
Lily and Eugene were looking for somewhere unusual for their wedding when someone told them about wedding parties at McDonalds. 'No one believed us but we thought it was a great idea!' Did their food come in heart-shaped boxes? 'No, nothing was different; there were hard chairs and square burger boxes but it was cheap and cheerful.'

2 ....
Some tourists were driving through Wisconsin when they noticed something large and rectangular in the thick branches of a tree. It was a blue and white pick-up truck. A local man put the pick-up truck there as a 'treehouse' for his son. 'Do you use anything to get up there?' asked the tourists. 'No,' he said, 'we climb the tree!'

3 ....
Overvecht station in the Netherlands isn't anywhere special but it now has a slide for passengers. 'It's long, straight and smooth and it's great fun! Everyone laughs when they slide down it. It gets them to the platforms really fast.' Does anyone miss their train? Not now!

A Slide to your ride

B The McWedding

C A car with a view

Comprehension

2 Read again and answer *True* (*T*), *False* (*F*) or *Doesn't say* (*DS*).

1 Weddings at McDonalds are cheap. [T]
2 The burgers were in heart-shaped boxes. ☐
3 Tourists in Wisconsin saw a truck in a tree. ☐
4 A local man made a treehouse for his son. ☐
5 There's a children's playground at every train station in the Netherlands. ☐
6 You can use the slide to get to the street. ☐

Vocabulary: Describing objects

3 **37** Listen and repeat. Make four lists under the headings *Size*, *Shape*, *Texture* and *Metal*.

bronze	gold	hard	large	long
rectangular	rough	round	silver	smooth
soft	square	straight	thick	thin

Size	Shape	Texture	Metal
large	*rectangular*	*hard*	*bronze*

4 Choose all the correct answers.

1 The trunk of a tree can feel ….
   a hard. **b** rough. **c** soft.
2 A box can be ….
   a round. **b** rectangular. **c** square.
3 Wedding rings are usually made of ….
   a gold. **b** silver. **c** bronze.
4 A slice of bread can be ….
   a thick. **b** smooth. **c** thin.

Grammar

Indefinite pronouns

Positive

Tourists noticed **something** large in a tree.
They were looking for **somewhere** unusual.
Someone told them about McDonalds.
Everyone laughs when they go down the slide.

Negative

No one believed us!
Nothing was different.
This road goes **nowhere**.
The station isn't **anywhere** special.

Questions

Does **anyone** miss their train?
Do you use **anything** to get up there?

5 Choose the correct words.

1 Eugene couldn't find a nice wedding ring for Lily *anywhere* / *nowhere*.
2 Eugene's mum didn't eat *something* / *anything* at the wedding!
3 *Someone* / *Anyone* helped the local man put the truck in the tree.
4 The local man saw a truck in a tree *nowhere* / *somewhere* in Virginia, too.
5 There's *nothing* / *anything* in guidebooks about the Overvecht slide.

6 Complete the text with the correct indefinite pronouns.

The Antikythera Mechanism

Over 100 years ago, in 1901, sponge divers were diving ¹ *somewhere* near the Greek island of Antikythera when they discovered an ancient shipwreck. On the ship they found a strange object – a hard lump of rock in a rectangular wooden box.

At first, archaeologists didn't think it was ² …………… important. But years later, when scientists looked more carefully, they discovered ³ …………… very special. Inside the rock were thirty bronze gear wheels, like a mechanical clock, and ancient Greek writing. Over 2,000 years old, it's the oldest complex gear mechanism in the world!

What was it for? ⁴ …………… knows for sure because there's ⁵ …………… like it ⁶ …………… else in the world. Today, scientists call it the world's oldest computer. They think it was ⁷ …………… for predicting eclipses of the sun and moon and deciding when to hold the ancient Olympic Games!

Speaking

7 Ask and answer about the Antikythera Mechanism to complete the information.

1 **A:** *What did the divers find?*
   B: *a hard lump of rock in a rectangular wooden box.*

1 What did the divers find?   4 Why is it special?
2 Where did they find it?   5 What was it for?
3 How old is it?

What	*a hard lump of rock in a rectangular wooden box*
Where found	
How old	
Why special	
What for	

8 Student A: go to page 101.
Student B: go to page 105.

> Now turn to Unit 3C in the Activity Book.

D Communication

Speaking: Make excuses and apologise

1 🅳🆅🅳 (1/38) **Listen and read.** *Today, the Jones family are going to lunch with Aunt Saffy.*

1

Mum: Hi, Tara! We're leaving for Aunt Saffy's in half an hour.

Tara: Sorry I'm late, Mum. I was watching a DVD with Fran and I didn't want to miss the end!

Mum: Never mind. Why don't you go and get ready?

Tara: OK. I'll be quick, I promise!

2

Tara: Mum, did you wash my blue dress?

Mum: Oh no! Sorry, Tara, I forgot.

Tara: Oh, Mum!

Mum: Can't you wear something else?

Tara: Hmm … Maybe. I'll look in my wardrobe.

3

Mum: Dylan, hurry up and change your clothes, please! Aunt Saffy's expecting us.

Dylan: Sorry, Mum, I'm not coming. Tom and I have got tickets for the rock concert, remember?

Mum: Oh, I forgot. Can you phone your aunt and apologise?

Dylan: All right. I'll do it now.

2 (1/39) **Choose the correct answers and complete the dialogues. Then listen and check.**

Dialogue 1

Mum: Fran! We're leaving for Uncle Jim's house in half an hour.

Fran: ¹ *I'm sorry I'm late*, Mum. I was doing my Art project when I saw the time.

    a I'll go now **b** I'm sorry I'm late **c** Never mind

Fran: Mum, did you wash my black skirt?

Mum: ² ....

    a Sorry, dear. I forgot. **b** Sorry, I can't. **c** All right.

Dialogue 2

Dad: Hurry up and change your clothes, Paul. Grandad's expecting us.

Paul: ³ .... I've got tickets for the football match.

    a I can't. **b** It's OK. **c** Sorry, I'm not coming.

Dad: Oh, sorry, I forgot. I'll tell Grandad you're sorry.

Paul: ⁴ .... I'll phone him.

    a It's OK. **b** I can't. **c** Sorry I'm late.

English today

- Sorry I'm late.
- Never mind.
- Sorry, (Tara), I forgot.
- Hurry up.
- Sorry, (Mum), I'm not coming.
- (Tom) and I have got (tickets for the rock concert).

Your turn

3 **Use the ideas below and Exercise 2 to help you write two dialogues. Then act them out.**

1 • leaving for Grandma's house in twenty minutes
   • visiting a friend
   • favourite jeans?

2 • Aunt Annie's expecting us
   • tickets for the football match

Writing: A letter of apology

4 Read the letter. Why did Lucy miss her uncle's birthday?

10 Lavender Close
Newport
NP10 5QR

12th November

Dear Uncle Julian,

How are you? I hope you and Aunt Marie are well and enjoying the good weather.

Thank you for inviting me to your birthday party last Saturday. I'm very sorry I couldn't come. I was in bed with flu. I was feeling really bad but I'm much better now.

By the way, thank you very much for sending me those DVDs. It was very kind of you. I really enjoyed watching them while I was in bed.

I'd love to see you soon. Can I visit you next weekend?

Please give my love to Aunt Marie.

Lots of love,

Lucy

5 Put the paragraphs of the letter in the correct order.

I hope you're well.

A _____

Give my love to your family.
With best wishes,
Paul

B _____

Thanks for inviting me to your house last Friday. I'm very sorry I couldn't come. I had to go to a friend's birthday party.

C _____

Dear David,

D | 1 |

Let's arrange to meet soon.

E _____

By the way, many thanks for lending me 'Photos from the Past'. It was very kind of you. I love books about photography and I really enjoyed reading it.

F _____

Writing tip

Structure of a letter

Greeting   *Dear (name),*

Paragraph 1 *How are you? I hope you're well.*

Paragraph 2 **Thanks**: *Thank you/Thanks for -ing*

   Apology: *I'm very sorry I couldn't ...*

   Reason: *I had tickets for an important game./I was in bed with flu.*

Paragraph 3 *By the way, many thanks for .../thank you very much for ... It was very kind of you.*

Paragraph 4 *I'd love to see you soon. Let's arrange to meet soon.*

Ending   *(Please) give my love/regards to ...*

   With best wishes,/All the best,/Yours,/Love,/Lots of love,

Look at Lucy's letter again and underline the phrases she uses from the list above.

Your turn

6 Use the information below to write a letter to your grandma. Use Exercises 4 and 5 to help.

• you couldn't go to your grandma's for Sunday lunch – you had to study for an important History test

• grandma sent you a cake – it made you feel better

> Now turn to page 37 in the Activity Book.

A great British author

What do you know about Dickens?

Charles Dickens

Ebenezer Scrooge (left)

Life

Charles Dickens was born in Portsmouth, England in 1812. When he died in 1870, he was Britain's favourite author.

Education

He didn't go to university. He only went to school for three years!

Early experiences

When he was twelve, his father went to prison because he couldn't pay his debts. Charles went to work in a factory. He used to work ten hours a day and earned six shillings (just 30p) a week. He described factory life and the life of the poor in many of his novels.

Novels

Dickens wrote twenty novels. He used to publish one chapter of a novel every week or month. The novels were popular and people used to wait impatiently for each episode – like soap operas.

Some of his characters' names became words in the English language. For example, Ebenezer Scrooge was a character in one of Dickens' stories. He hated spending money. Now, we use the word *scrooge* to describe a person who doesn't like spending money.

Write in and tell us about your favourite Dickens novel or character!

Pip with Miss Havisham in *Great Expectations*

My favourite Dickens character

My favourite character is Pip from 'Great Expectations'. Pip is an orphan and in the story he meets a girl called Estella and her rich guardian, Miss Havisham. Pip loves Estella but she doesn't love him because he has no money.

When Pip was a child he helped a man called Magwitch while Magwitch was escaping from prison. Years later, Magwitch gives money to Pip and makes him rich. In the end, Pip learns that friends are more important than money!

Penny, 13

New words

chapter debt episode escape
factory guardian impatiently
novel orphan poor prison
publish shilling

Reading

1 🔊 1/40 **Listen and read. Name two characters from Charles Dickens' novels.**

Comprehension

2 **Read again and answer the questions.**

1 How many years did Charles Dickens go to school for?
2 Why did Dickens work in a factory?
3 How much money did he earn in the factory?
4 How many novels did Dickens write?
5 Who was Ebenezer Scrooge?
6 Why doesn't Estella love Pip?
7 Who was in prison in *Great Expectations*?
8 What did Pip learn?

Listening

3 🔊 1/41 **Listen to the dialogue about a famous author and complete the text.**

Anna Sewell

Life: She was born in Great Yarmouth, England in ¹ _1820_ . When she died in 1878 she was living near Norwich in Norfolk.

Education: She only ² .... to school for two years! Her parents educated her at home.

Early experiences: She had an accident ³ .... she was walking back from school. Because of that she ⁴ .... to use horses a lot to help her get around. She loved horses and wanted people to be kind to them.

Novels: She only wrote one novel, *Black Beauty*. It is about the life of a beautiful black horse. ⁵ .... loved it.

Speaking

4 **Ask and answer about Michael Morpurgo. Use the information and the questions below.**

1 **A:** *When was he born?*
  B: *He was born in 1943.*

Michael Morpurgo

Life: Born in 1943, in St Albans, near London.

Education: Michael Morpurgo went to boarding school. He went to university at King's College in London.

Early experiences: His first job was a teacher in a primary school. First, he told stories to his class and then he started writing.

Novels: More than 100 novels. One very famous novel is *War Horse*, about a horse in World War I.

1 When was he born?
2 Did he go to university?
3 What was his first job?
4 How many novels has he written?
5 What is *War Horse* about?

Think about it

How often do you read books for fun? Do you spend more time reading from a computer screen or a book? What are some of your favourite books?

Project: A great author

5 **Find a picture of a great author from your country and write about him/her. Use the ideas below.**

- Life
- Education
- Early experiences
- Novels
- Your favourite character

Life
Miguel de Cervantes was born in Alcala de Henares in Spain in 1547... .

Education
Some people think he went to the University of Salamanca ... .

Early experiences

F Revision

1 Match 1–9 with a–i. Then complete the text below. Use the correct forms of the verbs.

1	start/leave	a	hard
2	do	b	a job
3	pass	c	successful
4	study	d	school
5	get	e	a living
6	earn	f	college/university
7	find	g	well
8	go to	h	a degree/diploma
9	become	i	exams

Emily's art

Emily [1] *started* school when she was five years old. She was a good student. She [2] .... very well and [3] .... all her exams. When she was eighteen years old she [4] .... to university. She [5] .... hard and [6] .... a degree in Art when she was twenty-two.

She had to [7] .... a living but she couldn't find a job as an artist. Emily also loved cooking so she [8] .... to catering college and [9] .... a diploma as a chef.

Then she had an idea: she started making 'art cakes'. They looked like famous paintings but they were cakes. People loved them! Soon she [10] .... successful and she opened her own shop. Well done, Emily!

2 Write sentences about what these people used to do when they were younger and what they do now.

1 *Fran's Mum didn't use to like cooking. Now she loves it.*

		Then	Now
1	Fran's mum:	not like cooking	love it
2	Fran's grandma:	live in Italy	live in the UK
3	Mr Jones:	go everywhere by bike	go everywhere by car
4	Mrs Jones:	wear only jeans	smart clothes
5	Tom's mum:	have a pet cat	have a pet dog
6	Tom's dad:	play football on Saturdays	play golf

3 Look at the table. Write about what these people could/couldn't do before they started school.

Dylan could swim and ride a bike. He couldn't … .

	Read and write	Swim	Ride a bike	Use a computer
Dylan	✗	✓	✓	✗
Tom	✗	✗	✓	✗
Tara	✓	✗	✓	✓

4 Tell Bruno what to do to complete the course.

1 *Walk along the wall.*

walk/the wall

swim/the pool

run/the tree

jump/the wall

walk/the table

jump/the box

jump/the box

run/the finish line

5 Complete the email with the past simple or past continuous forms of the verbs.

Subject: Surprise!

Hi Saffy,
Have a look at the photo that comes with this email. Here's the story. Last Saturday morning, Tara and Dylan [1] *were doing* (do) their household jobs. They [2] .... (tidy) the garage when they [3] .... (hear) a strange noise. It [4] .... (come) from a box behind the car. Tara was scared but Dylan wanted to see what was in the box. While he [5] .... (try) to open it, three mice [6] .... (jump) out. Dylan [7] .... (run) out of the garage faster than the mice!

6 Choose the correct words.

Dylan: Tara, have you got my MP3 player? I can't find it
¹ *somewhere /* (*anywhere*)

Tara: No, I haven't. It must be
² *somewhere / nowhere*
in your room.

Dylan: No, it isn't. I left it on the kitchen table before dinner. It was in a small blue bag. I found the bag but there's
³ *anything / nothing* in it. It's empty.

Tara: Well, maybe ⁴ *someone / anyone* took it from there. Why don't you ask Mum?

Dylan: I asked her. She said she didn't see ⁵ *anyone / anything* on the table before dinner.

Tom: Hi, guys! Oh, I love this song!

Dylan: Tom! Can I ask you ⁶ *something / nothing*? Is that your MP3 player?

Tom: No, it's yours. You gave it to me when I went running because I couldn't find mine!

7 Complete the dialogues with phrases a–i. Then act them out.

Dialogue 1

Mum: Hi, George! We're leaving for Aunt Tessa's in half an hour.

George: I ¹ *'m sorry I'm late* , Mum. I ² .... the football match on TV.

Mum: ³ .... Why don't you go and get ready?

George: OK. I'll be quick.

Dialogue 2

George: Mum, did you wash my black T-shirt?

Mum: Oh no! Sorry, dear. I ⁴ .... Can't you ⁵ ....?

George: OK. I'll look in my wardrobe.

Dialogue 3

Mum: Diana, ⁶ .... and change your clothes, please! Aunt Tessa's expecting us for lunch soon.

Diana: Sorry, Mum, I ⁷ .... My friends and I have got tickets for the pop concert, remember? You and Dad said it's OK.

Mum: Oh, I forgot. Can you ⁸ ....?

Diana: ⁹ .... I'll do it now.

a wear something else	**f** phone your aunt
b ~~'m sorry I'm late~~	and apologise
c All right.	**g** 'm not coming
d was watching	**h** forgot
e hurry up	**i** Never mind.

8 Choose the correct phrases to complete Nathan's letter to his uncle.

Dear Uncle Peter,
How are you? I hope you and Aunt Sarah are well.
¹ Never mind / (I'm very sorry) I couldn't come to your barbecue last Sunday. ² I had a bad cold / I couldn't.
It was awful at first but, fortunately, I'm ³ really sorry / feeling better now.
By the way, ⁴ thank you / I apologise for sending me the comic book. It was very kind of you. ⁵ I had great fun / Many thanks for reading it.
⁶ Lots of love / I'd love to see you soon. Why don't we meet next weekend? I could come and visit you.
All the best,
Nathan

Pronunciation: /ɪŋk/, /ɪŋ/

9 🕐 1/42 Listen and repeat.

I th**ink** that I'll s**ing**
A song about spr**ing**
And have someth**ing** to dr**ink**
That's fizzy and p**ink**!

10 🕐 1/43 Listen and circle the /ɪŋk/ sound. Then listen again and underline the /ɪŋ/ sound.

1 I think he's coming.

2 She's putting the dishes in the sink.

3 I've got nothing to wear. I've only got this pink T-shirt.

My progress

11 Read and tick (✓).

I can:	
talk about things that happened in the past but not now. *Jamie used to help in his parents' restaurant.*	☐
talk about abilities in the past. *He could cook when he was eight years old.*	☐
describe past experiences with *when* and *while*. *I was looking at the books when I heard a voice.*	☐
use prepositions of movement. *He walked across the road.*	☐
describe objects. *The box was large and rectangular.*	☐
make excuses and apologise. *I'm sorry I was late. I was watching a DVD.*	☐

> Turn to Unit 3 Check in the Activity Book on page 38.

4 The great outdoors

A Have you ever seen a bear?

Lesson aims:
• talk about survival skills
• talk about experiences in your life up to now

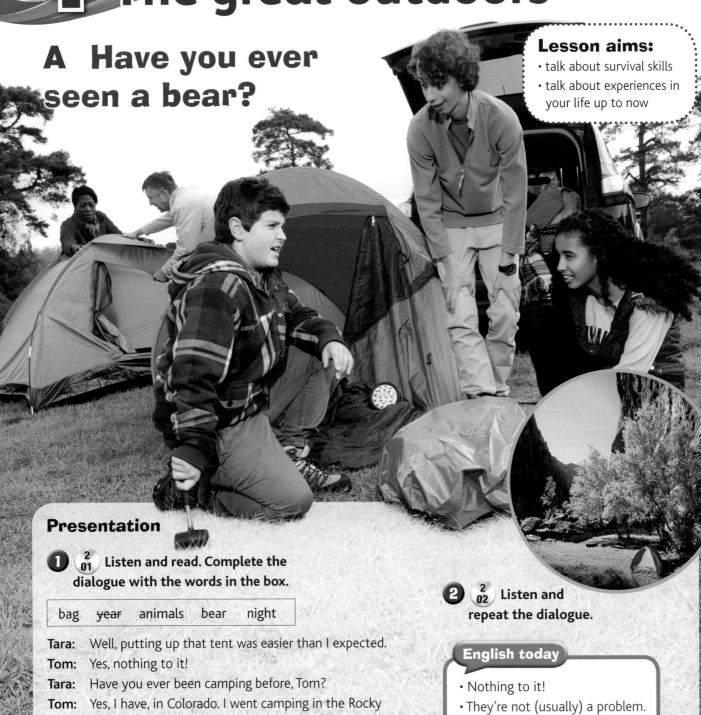

Presentation

1 🎧 2 01 **Listen and read. Complete the dialogue with the words in the box.**

| bag | ~~year~~ | animals | bear | night |

Tara: Well, putting up that tent was easier than I expected.

Tom: Yes, nothing to it!

Tara: Have you ever been camping before, Tom?

Tom: Yes, I have, in Colorado. I went camping in the Rocky Mountains National Park last ¹ _year_ with my dad and my brother. We camped near a river.

Dylan: Cool! But what about wild ² ....? Aren't there lots of bears there?

Tom: Yes but they're not a problem. If you light a fire, they'll usually stay away.

Tara: I'd really like to see a ³ ....! Have you ever seen one?

Tom: No, I haven't. Well, actually, I've never *seen* a bear but I've *heard* one.

Dylan: How do you mean?

Tom: Well, one ⁴ ...., a bear came right up to our tent.

Tara: Wow! Were you scared? What did you do?

Tom: Nothing! I hid in my sleeping ⁵ .... until it went away!

2 🎧 2 02 **Listen and repeat the dialogue.**

English today

• Nothing to it!
• They're not (usually) a problem.
• How do you mean?

Comprehension

3 **Read again and answer the questions.**

1 When did Tom go camping before?
2 Where did he go?
3 Are there wild animals there?
4 Did Tom see or hear a wild animal?
5 What did he do?

Vocabulary: Camping and survival skills

4 Listen and repeat. Complete the advert.

build a raft/shelter	put up a tent
catch a fish	read a map
cook (food) over an open fire	ride a horse
go camping/hiking/ horse-riding/rafting/ rock climbing/sailing	sail a boat
	see (a bear)
	sleep in a tent/ under the stars
light a fire	track wild animals

Wilderness weekends

Are you bored with the same old activities? Would you like to learn how to build a ¹ _shelter_ in bad weather, light a ² .... without matches and ³ .... a fish without a fishing rod? Then join one of our Survival Skills courses for twelve- to sixteen-year-olds!

We'll teach you how to ⁴ .... a map and ⁵ .... a raft to go down the river. You'll learn how to ⁶ .... wild animals and ⁷ .... your food over an open ⁸ .... But don't worry! You won't see a ⁹ ....!

You won't need to put up a ¹⁰ .... You'll sleep under the stars!

Sign up now!

Contact chloe@wildernessweekends.org

Grammar

Present perfect simple with *ever* and *never*

Have you ever **been** camping (before)?

Yes, I **have**. I **went** camping last year.

No, I **haven't**. I've **never been** camping.

Have you **ever seen** a bear?

Yes, I **have**. I **saw** a bear on holiday last summer.

No, I **haven't**. I've **never seen** a bear.

Choose the correct words.

We use *ever* / *never* for questions.

We use *ever* / *never* for negatives.

We add *-ed* to make the past participle of regular verbs, e.g. *cook-ed, join-ed, sail-ed*

! When you use *ever* or *never*, the past participle of *go* is *been*.

5 Listen to Tara and Fran's answers to the questions. Tick (✓) or cross (✗).

Are you a survivor?

Have you ever ...	Tara	Fran
1 slept under the stars?		✓
2 built a shelter?		
3 lit a fire without matches?		
4 cooked food over an open fire?		
5 done an orienteering course?		
6 been hiking in the mountains?		
7 seen a bear in the wild?		
8 ridden a horse?		

6 Complete the table of irregular verbs. Then listen and check.

Infinitive	Past tense	Past participle
build	built	¹ _built_
²	caught	caught
do	did	³ ....
go	went	gone/ ⁴ ....
have	⁵	had
⁶	put (up)	put (up)
ride	rode	⁷ ....
see	saw	⁸ ....
sleep	slept	⁹ ....

7 Ask and answer.

1 **A:** *Have you ever been camping?*

   B: *Yes, I have. I went camping last summer.*

      No, I've never been camping./I've never done that.

1 go / camping?	4 go to / the USA?
2 catch / a fish?	5 build / a raft?
3 go / on a plane?	6 see / kangaroo?

8 Tell the class about your partner.

Ferdinand has been camping. He went camping last summer.

Speaking

9 Student A: go to page 101.

   Student B: go to page 105.

10 Tell the class about your partner.

Paul has been to London. He's never slept in a tent.

> Now turn to Unit 4A in the Activity Book.

B Someone who takes risks

Lesson aims:
- describe people and their qualities
- define people, places and things

Steve Backshall – a man who takes RISKS!

Steve Backshall presents popular TV programmes about wildlife and natural history. He's travelled around the world and visited more than 100 countries. He's also written books that describe his experiences.

Steve is <u>passionate</u> about his work. Nature has always inspired him and 'the wild' is a place where he feels at home. He's an adventurous and fearless man who has taken a lot of risks. He's done some amazing things and has had some very scary experiences. He's caught giant spiders and dangerous snakes. He's dived with sharks, too. There's also a famous story about a crocodile that bit Steve while he was filming. Scary!

Steve is also passionate about rock and ice climbing so he has to keep himself fit and healthy. He's had some serious accidents but his injuries haven't stopped him. While he was rock climbing a few years ago, he fell and broke his back and his ankle and had to go to hospital. Two months later, he was filming his TV programme back in the wild! You can't stop him!

<u>Read more …</u>

Presentation

1 (2/06) **Listen and read. Name two scary experiences Steve has had.**

Comprehension

2 **Read again and answer _True_ (_T_) or _False_ (_F_). Correct the false statements.**

1   Steve presents TV programmes about history. _F_
    He presents TV programmes about wildlife and natural history.
2   He's been to more than 100 countries. ☐
3   He doesn't like being in the wild. ☐
4   He never takes risks. ☐
5   A crocodile bit him once. ☐
6   After his rock climbing accident, he stopped filming his TV programme. ☐

Vocabulary: Adjectives describing qualities

3 (2/07) **Listen and repeat. Which adjectives are in the text in Exercise 1? Underline them. What do you think they mean?**

active	adventurous	brave
careful	energetic	fearless
fit	healthy	inspiring
passionate (about)		strong

4 **Which three adjectives best describe you?**

Grammar

Defining relative pronouns: *who, that, where*

Steve is a man **who** has taken a lot of risks.

He has written books **that** describe his experiences.

The wild is a place **where** he feels at home.

Choose the correct words.

We use **who** for *people / places / things*.

We use **that** for *people / places / things*.

We use **where** for *people / places / things*.

5 **How quickly can you complete the definitions?**

1 A person who is ready to take risks is .._brave_..

2 A person who likes going to new places and doing new things is ....

3 A person who likes doing lots of physical things is ....

4 A .... is something that helps you find your way.

5 A .... is an animal that can live in the water and on the land.

6 Colorado is a place where you can see ....

7 A .... is the place where you go when you have an accident.

6 **Read the text and choose the correct words.**

Steve Backshall's parents inspired him to become interested in nature. He grew up on a small farm ¹ *who /* (*that*)*/ where* was full of rescue animals. Steve says he lived in a place ² *who / that / where* he had to milk all the goats and collect all the chickens' eggs before he went to school. There was a big sign outside his family's house ³ *that / who / where* said: 'Manure 10p a bag. Bring your own bags.'

Another man ⁴ *where / that / who* inspired Steve was Alfred Russel Wallace (1823–1913). Wallace was a British naturalist and explorer ⁵ *who / that / where* travelled widely in South America and Indonesia and studied the animals ⁶ *who / that / where* lived there.

Steve wants to inspire people ⁷ *where / that / who* don't usually watch wildlife programmes on TV. He's written books for children about saving wildlife. He hopes the people ⁸ *that / who / where* read his books will become passionate about nature, too.

Writing

7 **Who's Mike Perham? Complete the text to find out. Use *who*, *that* or *where*.**

Who's Mike Perham?

Mike Perham is a British teenager ¹ _who_ sailed solo around the world when he was only seventeen. Mike has written a book called *Sailing the Dream* ² .... describes his voyage.

Mike also drove solo around the world in a car when he was twenty. On this trip, he wanted to raise money for ShelterBox. This is an international charity ³ .... sends emergency shelter to help people survive disasters. Mike visited six places ⁴ .... the charity has sent help in the past.

Today Mike gives talks in schools about the things ⁵ .... happened to him on his journeys. He wants to inspire the school children ⁶ .... listen to his talks. He wants them to live their dreams.

Next Mike plans to *fly* around the world …

About you

8 **Write true sentences about you.**

1 I like people who …

2 I like going on holiday to places where …

3 I like TV programmes that …

> Now turn to Unit 4B in the Activity Book.

C Communication

Speaking: Talk about experiences up to now

1 **Listen and read.** *Dylan, Tara and Tom have signed up for a climbing course at the outdoor centre.*

1

Tara: This looks a bit scary.

Tom: Have you ever been climbing before, Tara?

Tara: No, never. But I've always wanted to try it.

Dylan: What about you, Tom? Have you ever been climbing?

Tom: Yes, I have, two years ago.

2

Tara: Oh, where were you?

Tom: In the Rocky Mountains.

Dylan: Was it a climbing wall like this one?

Tom: No, we climbed the real rock face.

Tara: No way! Was it scary?

Tom: Yes, it was very scary. I nearly fell off the rock face!

3

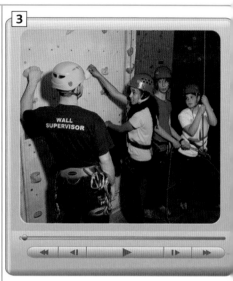

Instructor: OK, are you ready, kids? It's your turn now.

Tara: Oh no! Now I'm *really* nervous!

Tom: Don't worry, you'll be fine, Tara. There's nothing to it.

Tara: That's easy for you to say but I've never done it before.

Dylan: Come on, Tara! Up we go!

2 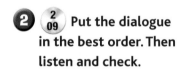 **Put the dialogue in the best order. Then listen and check.**

1	**Rob:**	This looks a bit scary.
	Rob:	Where were you?
	Anne:	Yes, I have, when I was on holiday last year.
	Anne:	Yes, it was brilliant.
	Rob:	Great! This is going to be fun.
	Rob:	No, never. But I've always wanted to try it. What about you? Have you ever done it before?
	Rob:	Was it a dinghy like this one?
	Anne:	In France.
	Anne:	Yes, it was.
	Rob:	Really? Did you enjoy it?
	Anne:	Have you ever been sailing before, Rob?

English today

- This looks scary/brilliant.
- Have you ever (been sailing) before?
- No, never./No, I've never done it before.
- But I've always wanted to try it.
- Where were you?
- Did you enjoy it?
- Yes, it was brilliant./No, it was awful.
- This is going to be fun.

Your turn

3 Imagine you and your friend are at a theme park. You're thinking about going on a rollercoaster ride. Use Exercise 2 to help you write a dialogue. Then act it out.

A: *This looks brilliant.*

B: *Have you ever been on a rollercoaster before?*

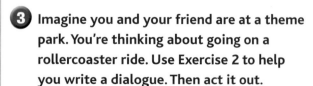

Writing: An interesting day out

4 Read the article Alec wrote for his school magazine and answer the questions.

Millennium Bridge and Tate Modern, London

A day in the city
by Alec Wood

Have you ever been on a trip to remember with your class? Last weekend, Year 8 went on a day trip to London. We took the train to Liverpool Street Station and the Underground to St Paul's Station.

First of all, we went inside St Paul's Cathedral. It's huge! Then, we crossed the Millennium Bridge over the River Thames and visited Tate Modern. It's an art gallery where you can see modern art. Some of the paintings were a bit weird! After that, we went to see the Globe Theatre where you can watch plays by Shakespeare. Finally, we visited an old prison called 'The Clink'. That was really cool but a bit scary!

Everyone enjoyed the day, especially the visit to 'The Clink', and nobody wanted to go home!

1 How did Alec's class travel to London?
2 In what order did they visit these places?
   Tate Modern ☐   The Clink Prison ☐
   St Paul's Cathedral ☐   The Globe Theatre ☐
3 What can you see at Tate Modern?
4 What can you do at the Globe Theatre?

Writing tip

Organising an article

Beginning Write a short introduction.

Middle Write about what happened. Use words to show the sequence of events: *When we arrived,/ First,/First of all, ... Then, ... After that, ... Finally, ...*

End Write a short conclusion.

Look at Alec's article again. Circle the words he uses to show the sequence of events.

5 Put the paragraphs of the text in the correct order. Then complete the text with words chosen from the box.

First	When we arrived	Finally
Then	After that	After lunch

A day at a theme park
by Janet Smith

A ☐ ¹ .... at Disneyland, we went for lunch at Planet Hollywood. Unfortunately, we didn't see anyone famous but the burgers were great.

² ...., we had a whole afternoon to go on all the rides. 'Big Thunder Mountain' was amazing.

B ☐ Disneyland is a place where everybody can have a great time. But one day isn't enough! Next time we're going to stay for a weekend.

C ☐ Last weekend, my family and I did something we've never done before. We went on a day trip to a different country! We went to Disneyland Paris by Eurostar. The train took us all the way there. It was a bit scary when it went through the tunnel under the sea but it was really fast.

Your turn

6 Imagine that you and your class went to the Woodland Centre last Saturday. Use the information below to write an article for your school magazine. Use Exercises 4 and 5 to help.

The Woodland Centre for Survival Skills
One-day Survival Course (Basic)
- Meet at 9.30.
- Walk from the coach park to the camp.
- Collect wood and light a fire.
- Learn how to build a one-man shelter.
- Prepare food and cook lunch over the fire.
- Walk in the woods and practise tracking animals.
- Return to the coach park at 5.30.

> Now turn to page 47 in the Activity Book.

myblog sign up   🏠 log in

AMAZING PLACES

My exciting expedition blog

Hi there, I'm Jade and I'm on a student expedition in Peru (South America). Follow my adventures here!

18th May, 07.38

I can't believe today is my last day in Peru. The time has flown!

This journey has been a wonderful experience. I've seen some amazing places and met some brilliant people who have inspired me.

I've done so many things on my trip. I've been white-water rafting on the Urubamba River and I've been hiking in the Andes Mountains. I've also fed llamas on a llama farm (they're so cute!). I've taught English to a group of children who live in a small traditional village and they've taught me a few words of Quechua (that's the language they speak). I've also made my own chocolate from scratch at the Choco Museum in Cuzco (and I've eaten it all!).

The place where I took the most photos is Machu Picchu. It's a city that the Incas built in the 15th century. It's high in the mountains and it's really spectacular.

Here's a map of Peru that has our journey marked on it. We've covered a lot of miles, as you can see!

I'll be sad to leave Peru tomorrow but it will be great to see my family and friends again.

Click **here** for more photos of my travels   **NEXT**

Llamas

Here's my itinerary:

1st–2nd days:	Arrival and sightseeing in Lima
3rd–5th days:	Go hiking in the Andes
6th–7th days:	Teach English to children in a village
8th day:	Go white-water rafting on the Urubamba River
9th day:	Visit Machu Picchu
10th–11th days:	Go sightseeing in Cuzco
12th day:	Departure

COLOMBIA
ECUADOR
PERU
Andes Mountains
BRAZIL
Urubamba River
Lima ★ village
Machu Picchu Cuzco
Pacific Ocean
BOLIVIA

New words

arrival	expedition	(my) own
century	flown (fly)	spectacular
cover	from scratch	traditional
departure	itinerary	

Reading

1 Listen and read. Find the places Jade talks about on the map.

Comprehension

2 Read Jade's blog again and look at her itinerary. Then ask and answer.

1 **A:** *Has Jade enjoyed the expedition?*
   B: *Yes, she has. It has been a wonderful experience.*
1 Has Jade enjoyed the expedition?
2 What did she do at the llama farm?
3 What did the children in the village teach her?
4 Where did she make her own chocolate?
5 What is Machu Picchu?
6 How many days did Jade spend hiking in the Andes?

> **Study tip**
>
> **Reading skills**
>
> You can guess the content of a text by reading its title.
>
> **Look at the titles on page 46 again. What do they tell you about the text?**

Listening

3 Listen and complete.

Zanskar river

A hot air balloon safari

Harry
• Where has he been?   ¹ *India*
• What's he done up to now?
  He's been ² .... down the Zanskar River.
• What's he going to do after this?
  He's going to help paint a ³ .... in a village.
Ellie
• Where has she been?   ⁴ ....
• What's she done up to now?
  She's been on a hot air balloon ⁵ .... at the Serengeti National Park. She's seen lots of
  ⁶ .... animals.

Speaking

4 Read the itinerary for an expedition to Iceland. B: Imagine you're in Iceland now and answer A's questions. A: Ask questions. What has B done?

A: *Have you been sightseeing in Reykjavik?*
B: *Yes, I have. I've visited the Reykjavik City Museum.*

Iceland expedition itinerary

1st–2nd days:	Arrival and sightseeing in Reykjavik. Visit Reykjavik City Museum. ✓
3rd day:	Hike to the top of a volcano. ✓
4th day:	See a geyser. ✓
5th day:	Go fishing. ✓
6th–7th days:	Go whale-watching. ✗
8th day:	Go scuba diving. ✗
9th day:	Departure

A geyser in Iceland

Think about it

Where in the world would you like to go on an expedition? Why?

Writing: An expedition

5 Write your own itinerary for an expedition. Choose a place and find some interesting things to do there. Include this information:
• where you want to go
• for how many days
• what activities you can do there
• what sights there are to see

6 Imagine you've been on the expedition. Write a blog entry about it.

> Hi there, I'm … and I'm on a student expedition in … . Follow my adventures here!

E Revision

1 Complete the text with the words in the box.

climb fish hiking light map rafting
shelter stars tents

FEARLESS!

Brenda Gill isn't afraid of danger. She can't be! In her job
she has to ¹ _climb_ mountains, go ² _____ across
deserts or sometimes go ³ _____ down fast rivers.
But she never reads the ⁴ _____ because she's the
person behind the camera on TV's *Survive the Wild*.

'At the end of the day we don't even put up the
⁵ _____,' she says. 'We don't have any! Usually we
build a ⁶ _____ or we ⁷ _____ a fire to keep
warm. Sometimes we catch a ⁸ _____ to cook.
Fortunately, I've never had insects for dinner!'

Does she love her job? 'Yes, I love sleeping under the
⁹ _____.'

**2 Ask and answer about Brenda Gill.
Use the prompts.**

1 **A:** *Has she ever climbed a mountain?*
  B: *Yes, she has.*
1 climb / a mountain?
2 be / scared?
3 hike / across a desert?
4 build / a shelter?
5 light / a fire?
6 have / insects for dinner?

3 Ask and answer the questions in Exercise 2.

1 **A:** *Have you ever climbed a mountain?*
  B: *Yes, I have. I climbed a mountain in the Dolomites
  when I was on holiday with my family.*

**4 Unscramble the adjectives. Then tick (✓) the
ones that describe Brenda Gill.**

1 usenturadvo   _adventurous_ ✓
2 tivace   _____ ☐
3 furelca   _____ ☐
4 lzay   _____ ☐
5 arlesfes   _____ ☐
6 itf   _____ ☐
7 althehy   _____ ☐
8 ysh   _____ ☐

5 Compete the crossword.

Clues

ACROSS

2 This is a place where you can see cows and chickens.
4 This is a small creature that has eight legs and can
  be scary.
5 This is an organisation that raises money to help
  people in need.
6 This is a kind of small sailing boat.
7 It's easy to have an ... when you're climbing in the
  mountains.
9 Tate Modern is an art ... where you can see modern art.
10 We can use these to light a fire.

DOWN

1 Steve Backshall is ... about nature and wildlife.
3 We can use this to catch fish.
8 This is something that you sleep in on a camping trip.

6 Complete the sentences with *who*, *that* or *where*. Then write *True* (*T*) or *False* (*F*).

1 The house __where__ Dylan and Tara live is in Cambridge. ☐T☐

2 Tom is the boy .... has come from the USA to stay with them. ☐

3 Chicago is the city .... Fran comes from. ☐

4 Jamie Oliver is a chef .... is famous for his wildlife programmes. ☐

5 A clock is a mechanism .... tells the time. ☐

6 The Eurostar is a train .... travels from London to Paris. ☐

7 Tate Modern is a place .... you can see traditional art. ☐

7 Complete the dialogue with the sentences below. There are three extra sentences. Then act out the dialogue.

Finn: This looks brilliant.

Molly: ¹ *Have you ever been horse-riding before, Finn?*

Finn: No, I haven't. But I've always wanted to try.

Molly: ² ....

Finn: Where were you?

Molly: ³ ....

Finn: Was it a riding school like this one?

Molly: ⁴ ....

Finn: Did you enjoy it?

Molly: ⁵ ....

Finn: Great! I'm going to enjoy this!

---

a Yes, I have.

b No, I went riding on the beach with my brother.

c I've never done that before.

d I have. I went riding when I was on holiday three years ago.

e It was a bit scary. But it was fun.

f Would you like to learn how to ride a horse?

g I was in Spain.

h ~~Have you ever been horse-riding before, Finn?~~

---

8 Read the introduction and conclusion of Tara's article. Then put the sentences in the middle paragraph in the correct order.

A day by the sea
by Tara Jones

Last weekend, my friend's dad drove us all to the seaside and I went sailing for the first time. I've never done anything like that before. I discovered that people who go sailing have to be fearless, fit and strong!

☐ It was the best weather for sailing.

☐ First, we found our boat and got on board.

☐ We were having a lovely time but suddenly the weather changed.

☐1 When we arrived at the seaside, it was sunny and a bit windy.

☐ After that, our sailing trip got really scary and I felt very sick.

☐ Then, we sailed out to sea.

Luckily, my friend's family are really good at sailing and we got back to land safely. But I won't do that again for a long time!

Pronunciation: the silent /r/

9 🎧 2 12 Listen and repeat.

There's a girl I know who sits on a swing.
She never speaks but she likes to sing.
It's the funniest thing you've ever heard –
She looks and acts just like a bird!

10 🎧 2 13 Say these words. Then listen and check.

1 world   2 work   3 earth   4 ever   5 learn
6 careful   7 fearless

My progress

11 Read and tick (✓).

I can:	
talk about survival skills. *Do you know how to build a shelter?*	☐
talk about experiences in my life up to now. *Have you ever been camping before?* *Yes, I have./No, I haven't. I've never been camping.*	☐
describe people and their qualities. *He's brave and energetic. She's fit and healthy.*	☐
define people, places and things. *He's a man who has taken many risks.* *Colorado is a place where you can see bears.*	☐

> Turn to Unit 4 Check in the Activity Book on page 48.

pick and mix

STAR SPOT

Shaun White, skating star!

Read and complete the fact file about Shaun.

Shaun White is a professional snowboarder and skateboarder. He's the only athlete who has ever won gold medals in the Winter *and* Summer X Games* in two different sports. He won gold medals in the 2006 and 2010 Winter Olympic Games. In the 2012 Winter X Games he got a 'perfect 100' score.

Shaun could skateboard when he was a child. The person who inspired him was his older brother, Jesse. Shaun wanted to do the best he could and be like Jesse and his friends. When he was six years old, Shaun started to snowboard. He won a lot of snowboarding competitions and became a professional at thirteen. He became a skateboarding 'pro' at seventeen.

Shaun has been very successful in his life. How does he do it? He says that it's all in the mind: 'You need to have a goal in your head all the time.'

* The X Games is an action sports competition in the USA.

Shaun's numbers:

2006/2010	*He won gold medals at the Winter Olympic Games.*
2012	....
6 years old	....
13 years old	....
17 years old	....

JUST JOKING!

Read the joke and answer the question.

What's the most amazing thing about the dog?

One day Jack saw an ad in the newspaper: 'Talking Dog for Sale. Call Bob.' Jack went to Bob's house and met the dog.

'Can you really talk?' Jack asked the dog.

'Please! I could talk when I was one month old!' the dog answered.

'This is awesome! Please tell me your story.'

'Well, I've had an interesting life. When I was a puppy I used to go to school with Bob. Then I went to university and I got a degree in Physics. In the end, I got a job with NASA but I missed my family so I came back home.'

Jack said to Bob, 'This dog is amazing! Why are you selling him?'

'Because he's a complete liar! Don't believe a word he says. He's never done any of those things!'

Quick Quiz

What type of traveller are you? Do the quiz to find out.

1 What kind of activities do you like doing when you're on holiday?

a Anything that's new and exciting – you love trying new things.

b Nothing too adventurous – you don't want to have any accidents.

c What activities? You're on holiday to relax!

2 You're on holiday with friends. They've decided to sleep under the stars. You say:

a What a great idea!

b Have we brought enough sleeping bags? Can we light a fire?

c Is there a hotel near here? I need a bed.

3 What's your ideal holiday?

a Somewhere amazing with lots of things to do.

b A place where you can relax but also have new experiences.

c Anywhere with a pool and a good restaurant – you don't want to do anything tiring.

4 Which of these holidays sounds awful?

a A beach holiday in a boring place with nothing to do or see.

b A holiday in a place you know nothing about.

c A hiking and camping holiday in the Amazon.

5 What's the first thing you pack for your trip?

a Your camera (or smartphone and charger). You want to have photos of all the exciting new places you're going to see.

b A guidebook and a map.

c A good book and a few magazines for the beach.

If you've got more As:
You're an **adventurous** traveller. You love seeing new places, meeting people and doing exciting things. You're the kind of person who enjoys travelling to unusual places.

If you've got more Bs:
You're a **careful** traveller. You enjoy having new experiences but you're not a person who takes risks. You like planning and you usually travel to places that you know you're going to like.

If you've got more Cs:
You're an **unadventurous** traveller. You want to have a quiet time and enjoy the sun, sea and a good meal. There's nothing wrong with that!

Guess what?

Who did what? Guess and complete the sentences with the names in the box.

| Elvis Presley | Steve Jobs | ~~Albert Einstein~~ |
| JK Rowling | Thomas Edison | |

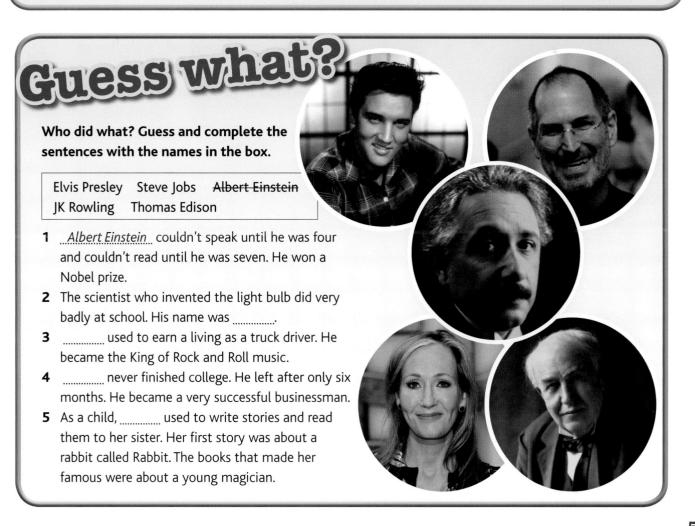

1 _Albert Einstein_ couldn't speak until he was four and couldn't read until he was seven. He won a Nobel prize.

2 The scientist who invented the light bulb did very badly at school. His name was ....

3 .... used to earn a living as a truck driver. He became the King of Rock and Roll music.

4 .... never finished college. He left after only six months. He became a very successful businessman.

5 As a child, ... used to write stories and read them to her sister. Her first story was about a rabbit called Rabbit. The books that made her famous were about a young magician.

5 Entertainment

A I've already seen it.

Lesson aims:
- talk about types of film
- talk about recent events with a present result

Presentation

1 (2/14) **Listen and read. What's on at the cinema tonight?**

Fran: It's Friday, what do you fancy doing tonight?

Tara: Let's go to the cinema. I haven't seen the latest Spielberg film yet.

Fran: Hmm ... what about a comedy or an action film? I'm not really into historical films.

Tom: And I've already seen it.

Dylan: I bet you haven't! It's only just come out.

Tom: Yes, I have. It came out in the USA two months ago.

Dylan: OK ... What else is on?

Tara: Well, there's a horror film. But it's got an 18 certificate so we can't see it.

Fran: Let's forget the cinema. Have you been to a school disco yet, Tom? There's one on tonight. It starts at 7.30.

Tom: No, I haven't.

Dylan: I'm not sure you'll enjoy it.

Tara: Of course he will. I bet you're a great dancer, Tom!

Tom: Well ...

Fran: If we all go it'll be a laugh.

Dylan: OK.

2 (2/15) **Listen and repeat the dialogue.**

English today

- What do you fancy doing (tonight)?
- I'm not really into (historical) films.
- I bet (you haven't)!
- Of course (you/he) will. • It'll be a laugh!

Comprehension

3 Read again and write *Dylan, Fran, Tara* or *Tom*. Who ...

1 wants to plan their evening?   *Fran*
2 wants to see the latest Spielberg film?   ....
3 doesn't like historical films very much?   ....
4 saw the Spielberg film two months ago?   ....
5 isn't sure the school disco is a good idea?   ....
6 thinks the disco will be fun?   ....

Vocabulary: Film types

4 (2/16) **Listen and repeat. Give examples of each type of film.**

Lord of the Rings *is a fantasy film*.

> action/adventure film   animated film/cartoon
> comedy   drama   fantasy film
> historical film   horror film   musical
> science fiction   thriller

Grammar

Present perfect with *just*, *already* and *yet*

Positive

The new Spielberg film **has just come** out.

I**'ve already seen** it.

Negative

We **haven't seen** the new Spielberg film **yet**.

Questions

Has Tom **been** to a school disco **yet**?

Yes, he **has**./No, he **hasn't**.

5 (2 17) **Say the past tense and past participle forms of these regular verbs. Then listen and check.**

1 arrive **2** ask **3** check **4** jump **5** visit **6** want

6 (2 18) **Complete the table of irregular verbs. Then listen and check.**

Infinitive	Past tense	Past participle
buy	¹ _bought_	bought
choose	²	chosen
come	³	come
find	found	found
meet	⁴	met
⁵	read	read
⁶	won	won

7 **Look at the pictures from the films. Match the titles with the pictures.**

1 *A*

1 Great Expectations **2** High School Musical **3** Pirates of the Caribbean **4** Avatar **5** Madagascar

8 **Write sentences about what has just happened in the pictures in Exercise 7.**

1 Magwich / find Pip / in the churchyard
Magwich has just found Pip in the churchyard.

2 Jake / meet Neytiri

3 Troy / win / the basketball championship

4 Jack Sparrow / jump / into the river

5 the animals / arrive / in Monte Carlo

Speaking

9 **A: You and your friend are planning to go to a film festival in London next Saturday. You're organising the trip.
B: You're A's friend. Ask A what he/she's done.**

B: *Have you checked the festival website yet?*

A: *Yes, I've already checked the website.*

B: *Have you ... ?*

A: *No, I haven't done that yet. I'm going to do it (tomorrow).*

> Things to do
> check festival website ✓
> find film listings and times ✓
> ask Dad and Mum for permission to go ✓
> choose films to see ✗
> book tickets for the films ✗
> check train timetable ✓
> buy train tickets ✗
> decide where and when to meet ✗
> buy a street plan of London ✓

10 **Student A: go to page 102.
Student B: go to page 106.**

About you

11 **Make a list of films that you're interested in. Which ones have you already seen? Which ones haven't you seen yet? Write sentences.**

I've already seen ... and ... . I haven't seen ... yet. I'm going to see it next week.

> Now turn to Unit 5A in the Activity Book.

B I've wanted to act since I was a child.

Lesson aims:
- talk about people in films
- talk about actions that started in the past

Presentation

1   Listen and read. Why is Ella in Los Angeles?

FILM FAN by Janine Reeve

This week Janine is in Los Angeles. She talks to Ella Vine, talented young actor and star of Nick Gordon's new film, *The Magic Crystal*.

HOLLYWOOD

Janine: Ella, you've lived here for over a year now. What do you think of life in LA?

Ella: I love it! I've always wanted to come to Hollywood. It's a dream come true!

Janine: You started acting professionally three years ago. How long have you wanted to be an actor?

Ella: I've wanted to act in films since I was a child. When I was at school, I used to make short films. I wrote and starred in them. My brother was the cameraman. He used my dad's video camera.

Janine: Who was the director?

Ella: My dad! He's always dreamed of making movies!

Janine: And now you play the main character in Nick Gordon's new fantasy, *The Magic Crystal*.

Ella: Yes, it's great to be in it. I've been a fan of Nick's for years! I saw my first Nick Gordon film when I was twelve. And now I'm here working with him! I can't believe it!

Janine: Do you miss your family in the UK?

Ella: I miss them a lot! I've been away from the UK for ages. I haven't seen my brother since April.

The interview continues on page 45.

English today
- It's a dream come true!   • I can't believe it!

Comprehension

2 Read again and answer *True* (T), *False* (F) or *Doesn't say* (DS).

1 Ella is in LA to act in a new film. ☐ *T*
2 She lives in a big house with a swimming pool. ☐
3 She lived in Hollywood when she was little. ☐
4 When she was at school she wrote her own films. ☐
5 Her father isn't a film director. ☐
6 She didn't use to like Nick Gordon's films. ☐

Vocabulary: Films

3 Listen and repeat. Match the words in the box with the people in the picture.

1 *She's a film star.*

People: actor   (film) star   character   cast   director   cameraman   make-up artist

What happens: plot/story   scene   special effects   ending

5

4 Complete with words from Exercise 3.

Film review

The Magic Crystal ★★★★⯪

The Magic Crystal, the exciting new fantasy film by director Nick Gordon, is finally here – and it's one of his best yet. British star, Ella Vine, is the only new face in a great [1] *cast* of Hollywood actors. She plays Helda, the main [2] .... in the film.

The Magic Crystal has the best [3] .... I have seen for a long time. The [4] .... where young Ella slowly changes into an old woman is really amazing!

The film is three hours long but you won't be bored! The [5] .... is full of surprises and you'll never guess the [6] ....! I recommend this entertaining and enjoyable film!

Grammar

Present perfect with *for/since*

Positive and negative
I've **wanted** to act in films **since** I was a child/**for** years.
I **haven't seen** my brother **since** April/**for** two months/**for** ages.

Questions
How long have you **wanted** to be an actor?
Complete with *for* or *since*.
... a long time   ... last week

5 Read Exercise 1 again and complete the sentences with *for* or *since*.

1 Ella has lived in LA *for* more than a year.
2 She's wanted to come to Hollywood .... a long time.
3 She's worked as a professional actor .... three years.
4 She's wanted to be an actor .... she was a child.
5 She's liked Nick Gordon's films .... she was twelve.
6 She's been away from the UK .... ages.

6 Look at Exercise 5. Ask and answer about Ella.

1 **A:** *How long has Ella lived in LA?*
  B: *She's lived in LA for more than a year.*

Listening

7 [2 21] Listen to the rest of the interview with Ella Vine and choose the correct answers.

1 When did you last see your mum and dad?
  a last April **(b)** last December
2 When did you last have a holiday?
  a two years ago **b** more than a year ago
3 How long have you lived in your house in Beverley Hills?
  a since August **b** for four months
4 How long have you had your dog, Snuggles?
  a for three weeks **b** since July
5 How long have you been a vegetarian?
  a since I was seven **b** since I was fifteen
6 When did you last have a cold?
  a seven years ago **b** after leaving school

8 Complete the sentences about Ella. Use your answers from Exercise 7, the present perfect and *for* or *since*.

1 She misses her mum and dad. She *hasn't seen them since last December*. (not see/them)
2 Right now she's busy with her career. She .... (not have/a holiday)
3 She lives in a lovely house in Beverley Hills. She .... (live/there)
4 She's got a dog, Snuggles. She .... (have/him)
5 She's a vegetarian. She .... (be/a vegetarian)
6 She's very healthy. She .... (not have/a cold)

Speaking

9 Ask and answer.

1 **A:** *How long have you lived here?*
  B: *I've lived here since (2007/I was five).*

1 How long / you / live / here?
2 How long / you / be / at this school?
3 How long / you / study / English?
4 How long / you / have / your (mobile phone/tablet/computer)?

About you

10 Write your answers to the questions in Exercise 9.

I've lived here since 2007.

> Now turn to Unit 5B in the Activity Book.

55

C I like hanging out with friends.

Presentation

1 Listen and read. What's the survey about?

myblog sign up   🏠 log in

What do you like?

Hi, I'm Danielle and I'm fourteen. I'm doing a survey on what teenagers like doing in their free time. Would you like to help? If you would, and you're aged between thirteen and nineteen, please do my questionnaire. Then come back and check out the results next month!

What's your answer to each question? Click from 1 to 5.
1 = love   2 = like   3 = don't mind   4 = don't like   5 = hate

Do you like ...

1 hanging out with your friends?	1 2 3 4 5
2 doing jobs around the house?	1 2 3 4 5
3 staying up late and watching DVDs?	1 2 3 4 5
4 instant messaging your friends?	1 2 3 4 5
5 staying in on Saturdays?	1 2 3 4 5

Which do you prefer doing? Click on it.
6 I prefer shopping in town to shopping online.
7 I prefer playing online games to playing board games.
8 I prefer going to the cinema to watching DVDs.
9 I prefer reading e-books to paper books.
10 I prefer chatting with my friends to texting them.

Add your comments here:

I don't mind babysitting my seven-year-old brother, David. My friends can't stand babysitting but I like looking after David. *Beth, 15*

I enjoy volunteering. I volunteer at an animal shelter every weekend. I want to find homes for all the animals there! I'd like to be a vet. *Mike, 16*

Comprehension

2 Read again. Ask and answer.

1 **A:** *How old is Danielle?*
  B: *She's fourteen.*

1 How old is Danielle?
2 What's the age group of the people in the survey?
3 What do the numbers 1–5 mean?
4 When are the results of the survey going to be ready?
5 Who hates babysitting?
6 Where does Mike volunteer?
7 What does he want to do?
8 What would he like to be?

Memory check: Free time activities

3 Listen and repeat. How often do you do each activity? Ask and answer.

A: *How often do you babysit?*
B: *I sometimes babysit for my aunt. What about you?*

babysit (for my parents/relatives)   chat online
do jobs around the house   hang out with friends
have a sleepover   IM (instant message)
make playlists   play (board/online) games
read books/e-books   shop (online)   stay in
stay up (late)   text (my) friends
volunteer (at an animal shelter)/do volunteer work
watch DVDs

Grammar

Verb + *-ing*
I **don't mind/like/enjoy/love**
hang**ing** out with friends.
I **hate/can't stand** do**ing** household jobs.

prefer
Do you **prefer** shopp**ing** online **or** shopp**ing** in town?
I **prefer** shopp**ing** in town **to** shopp**ing** online.

Listening

4 (2/24) **Listen to Tom and Tara doing another questionnaire. Write the correct numbers (1–5) or letters (a or b).**

1 = love   2 = like   3 = don't mind   4 = don't like   5 = hate

Do you like ...	Tom	Tara
1 having sleepovers at your house?	4	
2 cooking?		
3 doing sport?		
4 shopping for clothes?		
5 surfing the Internet?		
Do you prefer ...		
6 a hanging out with friends b staying in?		
7 a making your own playlists b downloading your friends' playlists?		
8 a texting your friends b talking on the phone?		
9 watching programmes a on TV b online?		

5 **Complete the text about Tom and Tara. Use your answers from Exercise 4.**

Tom loves [1] *doing sport*. He likes [2] .... He doesn't mind [3] .... but he doesn't like [4] .... and he hates [5] .... Tara and Tom prefer [6] .... to staying in. Tara prefers downloading her friends' playlists to [7] .... They both prefer talking [8] .... to texting their friends. Tom prefers watching programmes [9] .... but Tara prefers [10] ....

Speaking

6 **Do the questionnaire in Exercise 1 with a partner. Ask and answer.**

1 A: *Do you like hanging out with friends?*
  B: *I love hanging out with friends. What about you?*

6 A: *Which do you prefer, shopping in town or shopping online?*
  B: *I prefer shopping in town to shopping online. It's more fun.*

7 **Tell the class about your partner.**

(Sebastian) loves hanging out with his friends and staying up late. He hates doing jobs around the house.

Writing

8 **Write Daisy's blog profile. Use the information below.**

Name: Daisy, 13
Loves: [1] listening to music, [2] making playlists, [3] hanging out with friends
Can't stand: [4] doing nothing
Likes: [5] reading e-books
Enjoys: [6] travelling
Would like to: [7] travel around the world one day
Wants to: [8] volunteer at the local animal shelter

About me

My name's Daisy and I'm thirteen years old. I [1] *love listening to music* and [2] .... I've got the right playlist for any moment! I [3] .... but I [4] .... I always look for things we can do or places we can go. I [5] .... I already have thirty-eight e-books on my tablet PC. I [6] .... and I [7] .... Oh, and I also [8] .... because I love animals.

About you

9 **Make a list of the things you like/can't stand doing/would like to do. Then write your blog profile. Use the texts in Exercise 8 to help.**

Now turn to Unit 5C in the Activity Book.

Speaking: Express opinions

1   **Listen and read.** *Tom, Dylan, and Tara are choosing DVDs at their local library.*

1

Tom: This is a great film. Have you seen it yet?

Dylan: *Percy Jackson: Sea of Monsters?* Yes, I thought it was awful.

Tom: Really? Why?

Dylan: Well, the special effects were silly and the acting was terrible.

Tom: But the plot was brilliant and the ending was great!

2

Tom: *You* like action films, Tara. What did *you* think of it?

Tara: I agree with you, Tom. It was really entertaining.

Tom: See, Tara knows about films.

Tara: But *actually* I preferred the book. I've read all the books in the series. They were fantastic! Really great!

3

Dylan: I think Tara's right. I've read two of the books. They were really exciting.

Tom: I haven't read any of the books. Can I borrow one, Tara?

Tara: Sure. Hey, look at the time! We're going to miss *EastEnders* on TV. Let's go.

Tom: Oh no! Soap operas are rubbish!

2 **2 26** **Choose the correct answers and complete the dialogue. Then listen and check.**

Tara: Have you watched this DVD yet, Dylan? I thought it was brilliant!

Dylan: Yes, I have. I thought [1] *it was awful* .
   a it was awful   **b** I don't agree

Tara: Really? Why?

Dylan: I thought the plot was [2] .... and the special effects were terrible.
   a boring   **b** enjoyable

Tara: But the acting was fantastic and the ending was really [3] ....
   a silly   **b** moving

Dylan: [4] .... I thought it was rubbish.
   a Well, I don't agree.
   b I think you're right.

English today

- Have you seen/read/watched this film/book/DVD yet?
- I thought it was great/fantastic/brilliant/awful/rubbish.
- The special effects were amazing/awesome/excellent/silly.
- The acting was brilliant/terrible.
- The plot was exciting/enjoyable/entertaining/clever/boring.
- The ending was moving/great/silly.
- I agree./I don't agree.
- I think (you're/he's) right.

Your turn

3 **You and your partner are talking about a book you've read or a film you've seen. Use Exercise 2 to help you write a dialogue. Then act it out.**

A: *Have you seen/read ... yet?*

B: *Yes, I have. I thought ... .*

Writing: A book/film review

4 Read the book review and answer the questions.

The Hunger Games
by Suzanne Collins

The Hunger Games is a fantasy novel set in the future. It's about a teenage girl called Katniss who lives with her family in a village in the country. Every year, one boy and one girl from the village have to take part in the Hunger Games in the capital city. Katniss takes the place of her younger sister in the Games and wins against all odds.

I recommend this book because it's really exciting. Katniss is a brilliant character and she's very brave. The plot is clever and very entertaining. The ending is excellent, too. It's very moving. I'm going to read all the books in this series now.

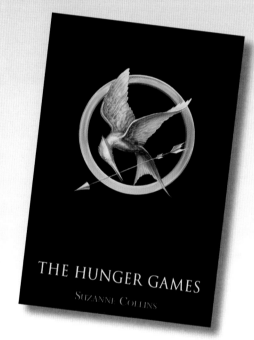

1 What kind of novel is it?
2 When is the novel set?
3 Who is it about?
4 What happens in the book?

Writing tip

Using adjectives

Use adjectives to express your opinion about a book, film, etc. in a review. There are lots of different ways to say that something is good or bad.

Look at Exercises 2 and 4. Find examples of adjectives that are positive and negative.

5 Read the film review. What's wrong with the second paragraph?

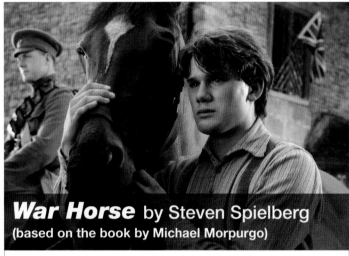

War Horse by Steven Spielberg
(based on the book by Michael Morpurgo)

This film is a drama set at the time of World War I. It's about a horse called Joey. A farmer buys Joey and he becomes great friends with the farmer's son, Albert. Unfortunately, Albert's father needs money and they have to sell Joey to the army. Joey goes to war and has many terrible adventures. Finally, at the end of the war, he finds Albert again.

I recommend this film to people who love adventure and care about animals. The story is very good, the cast *moving*
is good and the music is good. I think it's very good because the main character is a horse and we learn about horses in World War I. It's a very sad film but it has a happy ending.

6 Improve the second paragraph of the review in Exercise 5. Use the adjectives in the box.

brilliant	entertaining	excellent	great
interesting	~~moving~~		

Your turn

7 Write a review of a book or film that you have read or seen recently. Use Exercises 4 and 5 and the questions below to help.

Paragraph 1

1 What kind of book/film is it?
2 When/Where is it set?
3 Who is it about?
4 What happens in the story?

Paragraph 2

5 Why do you recommend the book/film?

Now turn to page 61 in the Activity Book.

THE MEDIA AND YOU

The whole world in your hands!

What do you think a teenager will say if you ask the question, 'What is your favourite type of media?' For years, that was an easy question to answer because up to now, teenagers have always chosen TV!

But perhaps that was because there weren't many other things to choose from. Most people could only choose from TV and the radio, books and magazines or newspapers. So for teens, TV was always the winner!

Now, if you read a recent survey, you'll see a change. Today, more British teenagers would miss the Internet (25 percent) than TV (18 percent). Why? Perhaps because online we can do most of the things we enjoy doing every day. We can catch up with our friends, listen to music, watch video clips, read the news or even watch our favourite TV programmes!

What else does the survey show? Did you know that most British teenagers have Internet access and a laptop at home? And almost half of them own a smartphone. Think about it – a smartphone is like a small computer which you can hold in your hand and use wherever you are. You can go on the Internet and connect to social networking sites (like Facebook and Twitter), download your favourite apps (games or dictionaries), take photos and send them to your friends, text, IM or email.

So, why has the Internet become so popular with teens? It's very simple really. Because it has brought the whole world into their hands!

FAST FACTS

British twelve–fifteen-year-olds who ...

- have a laptop at home: **93 percent**
- have the Internet at home: **95 percent**
- have a TV in their bedroom: **75 percent**
- have a smartphone: **41 percent**

New words

access   catch up (with friends)   (video) clip
media   popular   recent   social networking

Reading

1 (2/27) **Listen and read. What do teenagers use the Internet for?**

Comprehension

2 **Read again and complete the sentences.**

1 More British teenagers would miss the _Internet_ than TV.
2 Teens like watching video clips ....
3 Most British teenagers have Internet access at ....
4 .... of British teenagers own a smartphone.
5 You can use a smartphone to connect to social .... sites.
6 The Internet gives teenagers access to the ....

Listening

3 (2/28) **Listen to Jake, Maggie and Rick talking to a radio presenter about technology and the Internet. Choose the correct answers.**

1 Who has Internet access at home?
 a no one   **b** only Maggie   **c** all of them
2 Who has a laptop?
 a all of them   **b** only Rick   **c** only Jake and Maggie
3 How often do Maggie and Jake go online?
 a every day   **b** every week   **c** every weekend
4 Why does Jake go online?
 a to visit social networking sites
 b to watch video clips   **c** to do work for school
5 Who doesn't enjoy the Internet?
 a Maggie   **b** Jake   **c** Rick

Think about it

You can do lots of useful things on the Internet. Can you name some of them?

Speaking

4 **Do the questionnaire with your partner. Ask and answer.**

1 **A:** *Have you got Internet access at home?*
 B: *Yes, we have. We've had it for two years now.*

Using the Net!

1 **Have you got Internet access at home?**
2 **Have you got a laptop?**
3 **How often do you go online?**
4 **How many hours a day do you spend online?**
5 **Why do you go on the Internet? Number from 1 (most important) to 7 (least important)**

☐ find information/schoolwork
☐ visit social networking sites
☐ listen to music
☐ read the news
☐ IM/chat with friends online
☐ play games
☐ watch funny video clips

Writing

5 **Do the questionnaire in Exercise 4 with three more people in your class. Then write a report.**

- Our survey has shown that .... percent of our classmates have got Internet access at home.
- .... of them have got a laptop.
- They usually go online ... .
- They spend around ... .
- They go on the Internet because ... .

F Revision

1 Match the definitions (1–6) with the film types (a–f).

1 *b*

1 A film that makes you laugh.
2 A film that makes you feel very scared.
3 A film that has lots of songs in it.
4 A film that has lots of exciting events in it, for example car chases.
5 A film that tells an exciting story about crime and criminals
6 A film about life in the future

a a science fiction film
b a comedy
c an action/adventure film
d a horror film
e a thriller
f a musical

2 Complete the text with the words in the box.

cast   director   ~~film star~~   make-up artist
scene   story

Be in *Next Door Mates* for a day!

Have you ever wanted to be a ¹ *film star*? Well, here's your chance to star in a soap. Join the ² .... of the popular soap opera *Next Door Mates* for a day!

What do you have to do? Simply write a ³ .... for a future episode of our entertaining TV series. It must fit the ⁴ .... so far.

The lucky winner will visit our best ⁵ .... and then have lunch with the ⁶ .... of the show and all the actors. And he or she will go on TV for millions to see!

For more information, contact jane@ndm.ytv.com

3 Dylan is very busy this weekend. Read his 'To do' list and write sentences. Use the present perfect and *already* or *yet*.

1 Dylan *hasn't done his homework yet*.
2 He's *already* ....
3 ....
4 ....
5 ....
6 ....

> To do
> 1 do my homework ✗
> 2 tidy my room ✓
> 3 walk the dog ✗
> 4 buy a ticket for the concert next week ✓
> 5 phone Alan about the History project ✗
> 6 watch 'Wildlife Special' on TV ✓

4 Read Dylan's 'To do' list again. Ask and answer.

1 A: *Has Dylan done his homework yet?*
   B: *No, he hasn't./No, he hasn't done that yet.*
   A: *Has he ... yet?*
   B: *Yes, he's already done that.*

5 Complete the email with *just, already, yet, for* or *since*.

Colorado Rockies

Subject: My news   send   save

Hi Gary,

I've ¹ *just* received your postcard – thanks! Have you caught any fish ² ....? I've been in Cambridge ³ .... three months now and I'm really enjoying it.

I've visited London three times ⁴ .... September. I've ⁵ .... visited all the best museums. I haven't been on the London Eye ⁶ .... and I haven't done any shopping but I will.

Have you done all the things on your list ⁷ ....?

Oh, Mrs Jones has ⁸ .... shouted up the stairs. Dinner's ready. I'll write again soon.

Bye for now,
Tom

P.S. I've been in the rugby team ⁹ .... I arrived. So far this year we've won every match!

6 Complete the interview with Marvin Hopper. Use the present perfect. Then act it out.

Q: [1] How long / you / live / in the UK?
How long have you lived in the UK?

Marvin: [2] I / live / in the UK / 2005

Q: [3] How long / you / be / a film director?

Marvin: [4] I / be / a film director / ten years

Q: [5] How many films / you / make?

Marvin: [6] I / (already) make / three science fiction films / But I / not make / a horror film (yet)

7 Complete the dialogues with sentences a–i. There are three extra sentences.

1 **A:** Have you seen the new film at the Picture House? What a great film!

B: [1] *I don't agree. I thought it was awful.* The acting wasn't very good and the ending was silly!

2 **A:** I've read lots of the Jacqueline Wilson books and they were great.

B: [2] .... I really enjoyed reading them, too.
[3] ....

3 **A:** I watched *Superman the Movie* on DVD last night. It's a terrible film!

B: [4] .... But the special effects were very good for 1978.

4 **A:** Wow! I've just seen the new Nick Gordon film. It was amazing!

B: [5] .... But I can't stand the actor who plays Ella Vine's father. [6] ....

---

a ~~I don't agree. I thought it was awful.~~
b They're very boring.
c I think the film is OK.
d His acting is terrible.
e I think you're right.
f I don't agree. I thought it was brilliant.
g Well, I agree the plot is a bit silly.
h What's it about?
i They're very entertaining.

---

8 Read the sentences. Choose the correct words to replace the underlined adjectives.

1 The plot was really good. I didn't expect the ending. It was a big surprise! **(a)** clever **b** boring

2 The film had good special effects. They looked real!
a ugly **b** amazing

3 The actor who played the main character was good. It was the best acting he's ever done. **a** OK **b** brilliant

4 This horror film didn't frighten me at all! The acting was bad and a lot of the scenes were bad.
a terrible **b** great / **a** silly **b** scary

5 This film wasn't very good. In fact, I was bored.
a funny **b** interesting

Pronunciation: /t/, /d/ before a consonant

9 🎧 2 29 Listen and repeat. Can you hear all the underlined letters?
I haven't done my homework yet.
I've just told my friend to wait.
Mum's just turned the oven on!
How long will my food take?

10 🎧 2 30 Listen and circle the letter that you can't hear in each underlined pair.
1 Don't touch that button!
2 He's just driven a hundred miles!
3 I didn't drop the bag!
4 Where did you find that hat?

My progress

11 Read and tick (✓).

I can:	
talk about types of film. *I don't like horror films but I like comedies.*	☐
talk about recent events with a present result. *The new Spielberg film has just come out.*	☐
talk about people in films. *She's a talented actor.*	☐
talk about actions that started in the past. *How long have you lived here? Since 2001.*	☐
talk about likes, dislikes and preferences. *I prefer shopping in town to shopping online.*	☐
express opinions. *I don't agree. I thought it was great/brilliant.*	☐

> Turn to Unit 5 Check in the Activity Book on page 62.

Rules and advice

Lesson aims:
- talk about obligation
- talk about permission
- talk about family rules

A I have to be home by 8.00.

Presentation

1 (2/31) **Listen and read. What does Tara hate doing?**

Tara and her friend, Erin, are chatting online.

Tara: Hey, Erin. What are you up to?

Erin: Hi! I've just finished tidying my room. ☺

Tara: Cool. Do you want to go to the new ice rink tomorrow? Everyone says it's really cool!

Erin: Sure! And then let's go for a pizza.

Tara: Sorry, I can't. I'm not allowed to stay out late. I have to be home by 8.00.

Erin: You're kidding! But tomorrow's Saturday! Do you have to be home by 8.00 on Saturdays, too?

Tara: Oh, I forgot! It's OK, then. I'm allowed to stay out until 10.00 at weekends. ☺

Erin: Me too! And I don't have to be back until 11.00 if I'm at a party!

Tara: Lucky you. Last Saturday I got home late from Sandra's party and my parents were really angry. I had to stay in all day Sunday and I wasn't allowed to watch TV or use my laptop! ☹

Erin: Wow! That's strict!

Tara: Tell me about it! I *hate* sitting around and doing nothing!

Erin: Anyway, I'm off to my dance class. See you tomorrow.

2 (2/32) **Listen and repeat the dialogue.**

> **English today**
> - What are you up to?
> - You're kidding!
> - Lucky you.
> - That's strict!
> - Tell me about it!
> - I'm off (to my dance class).

Comprehension

3 **Read again and answer *True* (T) or *False* (F).**

1 Tara can't go to the ice rink tomorrow. `F`
2 Erin wants to have a pizza after the ice rink. ☐
3 Tara can't stay out later than 8.00 on weekdays. ☐
4 Erin can stay out until 11.00 every day. ☐
5 Tara was at a party last Saturday. ☐
6 Tara has never been home late. ☐

Memory check: Household jobs

4 **Complete with the verbs in the box.**

clear	do	feed	lay	load	~~make~~	tidy
vacuum	walk	water				

1 *make* my bed
2 .... my room
3 .... the table
4 .... my room
5 .... the table
6 .... the washing-up
7 .... the dishwasher
8 .... the dog
9 .... the plants
10 .... the dog

Grammar

***have to* – present simple**

Positive and negative

I **have to** be home by 8.00.

I **don't have to** be back **until** 11.00.

Questions

Do you **have to** be home by 8.00?
Yes, I **do**./No, I **don't**.

***have to* – past simple**

Positive

I **had to** stay in all day Sunday.

5 **Complete the sentences with the correct form of *have to* and the phrases on the board.**

> do washing-up: Dylan   **have to study for a test!**
>
> walk the dog: Dad   sorry! have to stay late at work
>
> vacuum the living room: Tara   have to go to choir practice!
>
> water the plants: Mum   have to visit Aunt Saffy!

1 Dylan _has to do the washing-up_ after dinner. Yesterday he _had to study for a test_ so Tara did it for him.

2 Dad .... every evening. Yesterday .... so Mum did it for him.

3 Tara .... on Saturdays. Last Saturday .... so Dylan did it for her.

4 Mum .... every Sunday. Last Sunday .... so Dad did it for her.

6 **Ask and answer about things you have to do at home.**

1 **A:** *Do you have to do the washing-up?*
   B: *Yes, I do./No, I don't.*
   I have to do the washing-up every day./I don't have to do the washing-up.

1 do the washing-up

2 tidy your room

3 study hard for tests

4 play your music quietly

5 tell your mum where you're going

Grammar

be allowed to

Positive and negative

I**'m allowed to** stay out until 10.00 at weekends.

I**'m not allowed to** stay out late.

Questions

Are you **allowed to** be back later than 8.00 on Saturdays? Yes, I **am**./No, I**'m not**.

7 **Ask and answer about what you are and aren't allowed to do.**

1 **A:** *Are you allowed to stay out late?*
   B: *I'm not allowed to stay out late on weekdays … .*

1 stay out late

2 watch TV after ten o'clock

3 chat with your friends on the Internet

4 go to sleepovers

5 have the hairstyle you like

Listening

8 **2 33** **Listen to Tom and Dylan talking about family rules. Answer *True* (*T*), *False* (*F*) or *Doesn't say* (*DS*).**

1 Dylan has to ask his parents if he wants to go out. [T]

2 Tom and Dylan always have to say where they're going and who with. [ ]

3 Tom has to be home by ten o' clock on weekdays. [ ]

4 Dylan isn't allowed to go out on weekdays. [ ]

5 Dylan has to call his parents and explain why he's going to be late. [ ]

6 Tom goes to bed at ten o'clock on weekdays. [ ]

7 Dylan is allowed to stay up until ten o'clock on weekdays. [ ]

Writing

9 **Write about your family's rules.**

> My family's rules
> Family rules are important in our house. I have to help my mum with the shopping on Saturdays. I don't have to … . I'm allowed to … . I'm not allowed to … .

> Now turn to Unit 6A in the Activity Book.

B You should call an ambulance.

Lesson aims:
- talk about injuries and illnesses
- give advice about treatment

Presentation

1 Listen and read. Choose the correct words.

First aid facts

No idea about first aid? Then read this leaflet!

What should you do ...

if someone has a bad fall?

First, ask where it hurts. If you think the person has broken a leg or an arm, you should call an ambulance and keep the person ¹ warm / cool. You shouldn't move the person.

if someone faints?

Raise the person's ² arms / legs higher than their head – use a ³ table / chair or a cushion. Keep the person cool. A person who has fainted shouldn't stand up too quickly.

if someone sprains their ankle?

You should raise the ankle and put a(n) ⁴ ice / heat pack on it. Ice burns, so you shouldn't put the pack next to the skin. Put a bandage on the ankle but the person should ⁵ take it off / wear it at night.

Comprehension

2 Read again and choose the correct answers.

1 Call an ambulance for somebody who has ...
   a fainted.   b broken their arm.

2 Don't move a person who has ...
   a had a bad fall.   b sprained an ankle.

3 You can help a person who has fainted by ...
   a lifting their legs.   b lifting their head.

4 After you have fainted, stand up ...
   a slowly.   b quickly.

5 The best thing for a sprained ankle is ...
   a a massage.   b an ice pack.

6 A bandage helps a sprained ankle ...
   a at night.   b during the day.

Vocabulary: Injuries, illnesses and treatments

3 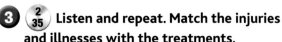 Listen and repeat. Match the injuries and illnesses with the treatments.

Injuries and illnesses
break your arm/leg   catch/have a stomach bug
cut yourself   faint   have sunburn
pull a muscle   sprain your ankle/wrist

Treatments
call an ambulance   clean it   drink lots of water
keep (it) cool/warm   put a bandage on it
put cream on it   put an ice pack on it
put a plaster on it   rest

break your arm or leg – call an ambulance, keep warm

4 **Complete the dialogue. Use Exercise 3 to help.**

Tara: Tom, have you ever had a sports injury?

Tom: Yes, I [1] _broke_ my leg when I was skiing five years ago and I've [2] .... my right ankle three times playing basketball. The last time I did it, I had to wear a [3] .... for a month.

Tara: Have you ever had any serious illnesses?

Tom: Well, I was on holiday in Costa Rica once and I caught a [4] .... bug. Mum had to [5] .... an ambulance and I spent the holiday in hospital.

Tara: Have you ever [6] ....?

Tom: Well, yes, but just once. I was standing in the sun too long. I had to lie with my legs raised for half an hour.

Tara: Wow! You've had some adventures!

About you

5 **Write a list of injuries or illnesses you have had. What treatments did you have?**

I sprained my ankle two years ago when I was (playing football). My mum put a bandage on it and I had to rest for a few days.

I cut my finger when I was (helping Mum chop vegetables for dinner). I cleaned the cut and put a plaster on it.

Grammar

should/shouldn't

Positive

You **should** call an ambulance.

You **should** put an ice pack on it.

The person **should** take it off at night.

Negative

You **shouldn't** move the person.

They **shouldn't** stand up too quickly.

Questions

What should I do if someone faints?

Should I call an ambulance?

Yes, you **should**./No, you **shouldn't**.

6 **Imagine these things have happened. What should you do?**

1 Your friend has fainted.

I should raise his/her legs and keep him/her cool.

2 You sprain your ankle.

3 Your little brother has cut his knee.

4 You catch a stomach bug.

5 Your friend falls and breaks his/her leg.

6 You have sunburn.

Speaking

7 **A: Imagine you're going on holiday to India. Ask for advice.**

B: Give advice. Use the information below.

A: _Should I drink bottled water?_

B: _You should always drink bottled water. You should never drink tap water._

Travelling to India on holiday?

Frequently asked questions	
Should I …	**You should …/You shouldn't …**
drink bottled water?	always drink bottled water. ✓
	never drink tap water. ✗
visit places at midday?	never go out in the midday sun. ✗
	only go out in the morning and late afternoon. ✓
What should I do if I …	**You should …/You shouldn't …**
get a stomach bug?	drink lots of bottled water. ✓
	eat spicy food. ✗
get sunburn?	put cream on and keep cool. ✓
	stay in the sun ✗

8 **Student A: go to page 102.**

Student B: go to page 106.

9 **Imagine a friend is coming to visit your country. Write five things they should and shouldn't do.**

> Now turn to Unit 6B in the Activity Book.

Communication

Speaking: Give advice

1   **Listen and read.** *Tara is asking her mum for advice.*

1

Tara: Mum, don't tell Dylan but I wore his favourite T-shirt yesterday and I got tomato ketchup all over it. What should I do?

Mum: Why don't you wash it first and then we'll see?

Tara: I *have* washed it but it hasn't come off!

2

Mum: Mmm. I think you'd better tell him about it, Tara.

Tara: But he'll be angry with me!

Mum: Well, I think you should apologise. You know you shouldn't take his clothes without asking.

Tara: Oh, all right, but what about the T-shirt?

3

Mum: You could buy him a new T-shirt with your pocket money.

Tara: But they cost £20!

Dylan: You should stop taking my clothes, then!

Tara: Oops! Hi, Dylan! Look, I'm really sorry.

2 **2/37** **Complete the dialogue with a–e. Then listen and check.**

Dylan: Dad, I borrowed Tara's MP3 player yesterday and now it doesn't work. ¹ *What should I do?*

Dad: ² .... to the shop?

Dylan: I have. They can't fix it!

Dad: ³ .... Tara what's happened.

Dylan: But she'll be angry with me!

Dad: ⁴ .... and promise not to take her things again without asking.

Dylan: All right but what about the MP3 player?

Dad: ⁵ ....

Dylan: But they cost £50!

a You could buy her a new one.
b Then you'd better tell
c Why don't you take it
d ~~What should I do?~~
e Well, I think you should apologise

English today

• What should I do?
• Why don't you ... ?
• I think you'd better ...
• I think you should ...
• You could ...

Your turn

3 **A: You borrowed your brother's mobile phone without asking. Now it's stopped working. Ask B for advice. B: Give A advice. Use Exercise 2 to help you write the dialogue. Then act it out.**

A: *Paolo, I borrowed Mario's mobile phone without asking. Now it doesn't work. What should I do?*

B: *Well, why don't you ...*

Writing: A problem page

4 Read Nathan's email and Amy's reply. What's Nathan's problem?

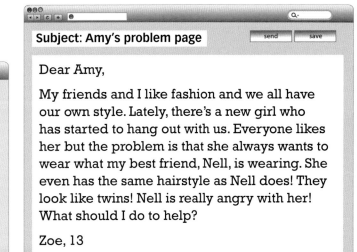

Subject: Amy's problem page

send   save

Dear Amy,

My family and I moved to a new town last month so I have to go to a new school. I had a lot of friends in my old town and I'd like to make new friends here. However, my problem is that I'm a bit shy. Talking to people I don't know isn't easy for me. Can you please help? What should I do?

Nathan, 14

Subject: Re: Amy's problem page

Dear Nathan,

To begin with, you should try to make friends from your class. Find a reason to talk to someone. For example, why don't you ask a classmate to explain something about your homework? It's a great way to start talking.

You could also join a club or start playing a sport. People who have the same interests make friends a lot more easily. Finally, don't forget to smile as it makes everyone like you! Good luck!

Amy

Writing tip

Linking words
Use linking words to join sentences and ideas.

Look at Exercise 4 and circle these linking words and phrases.

To begin with, ...   Finally, ...   However, ...
For example, ...

---

5 Read the emails and choose the correct words.

Subject: Amy's problem page

send   save

Dear Amy,

My friends and I like fashion and we all have our own style. Lately, there's a new girl who has started to hang out with us. Everyone likes her but the problem is that she always wants to wear what my best friend, Nell, is wearing. She even has the same hairstyle as Nell does! They look like twins! Nell is really angry with her! What should I do to help?

Zoe, 13

Subject: Re: Amy's problem page

Dear Zoe,

¹ *Finally /(To begin with)*, you should calm Nell down. ² *However / For example*, you could tell her that being angry doesn't help. People can wear what they want!

³ *However / Finally*, there are a few more things you could do. ⁴ *For example / However*, you could tell your new friend that you would like to help her. You could offer to go shopping with her and help her choose her clothes. ⁵ *To begin with / Finally*, don't forget to tell her how special she looks – I'm sure she'll love her new style!

Best wishes,

Amy

Your turn

6 Write to Amy with a problem. Use the emails in Exercises 4 and 5 and the ideas below to help. Then swap with a friend.

Dear Amy,

My little brother/sister always borrows my favourite clothes without asking. ...

• favourite jacket
• left it in the rain
• dirty and torn

Imagine you're Amy. Reply to your friend's email with your advice. Don't forget to use the correct linking words.

> Now turn to page 71 in the Activity Book.

HEALTH AND EXERCISE

Tyler says ... be a HEALTHY teenager!

Teenagers should do sixty minutes of exercise every day.

Why?

1 Your body will produce endorphins. These are chemicals inside the body which make you happier and more relaxed.
2 You'll sleep better.
3 Your bones will get stronger.
4 You'll look better. (Exercise tones your muscles and helps you stay a healthy weight.)

Tyler's top tips:

- Exercise should never be boring, so choose something which you enjoy.
- Always warm up before you exercise. Cold muscles can cause injuries.
- Always do some stretching after exercise.
- Eat a healthy snack two hours before you exercise.
- If you want a good exercise routine, you should do some aerobic exercise, build muscles and do some stretching.

Aerobic exercise makes your heart beat faster. This means your heart is working and getting stronger – the heart is a big muscle, too! Most team sports – football, hockey and basketball – are great aerobic exercise. But running, swimming and skating are aerobic, too.

It's important to **build muscles**. Strong muscles allow you to exercise for longer. They also protect your bones from accidents and injuries. And muscle burns more calories than fat. Rowing and push-ups build arm muscles. Running and cycling are great for leg muscles and rowing and pilates exercise your stomach muscles.

Stretching helps your body become more flexible, so you can move better. If your body is flexible, you won't pull a muscle or sprain an ankle. Martial arts and dancing are great for becoming flexible.

New words

aerobic   bone   burn   calorie   chemicals
endorphins   flexible   heart   protect
push-up   stretching   tone   warm up

Reading

1 🔊 2/38 **Listen and read. Complete with the correct sports.**

1 Exercises the heart	_football,_ ....
2 Exercises the arms	.... _push-ups_
3 Exercises the legs	....
4 Exercises the stomach	....
5 Improves flexibility	....

Comprehension

2 **Read again and answer the questions.**

1 Who is this text for?
2 How much exercise should teens do?
3 What do endorphins do?
4 What two things should you do before exercise?
5 What should you do after exercise?
6 What protects your bones from accidents and injuries?
7 How does stretching help?

Study tip

Don't worry about new words. Try to understand them from the context. Underline them and check them later in a dictionary.

Match the words from the text with their meanings (a–c).

flexible   push-ups   heart

a arm exercises which build muscle
b a large muscle inside the body
c You are this if your body moves easily.

Listening

3 2/39 **Listen and complete the information.**

Green Bridge Leisure Centre facilities

50-metre heated [1] _swimming pool_ :
Open: 7.00 a.m. to [2] .... daily.
Closed: 12.00 to 1 p.m. on [3] ....
for swimming lessons.

Six indoor [4] .... courts:
Book in advance for one hour.

Gym: (over [5] .... only)
Open: 7.00 a.m. to 9.00 p.m. daily.
Aerobics, yoga or pilates six times a day.

Family membership:
Price: £50 a month, £300 a [6] ....

Speaking

4 **Ask and answer about keeping fit and healthy. Use these questions.**

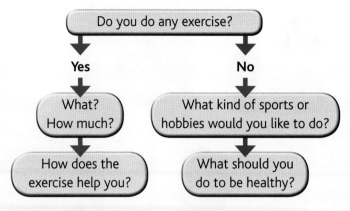

Do you do any exercise?

Yes — No

What? How much? — What kind of sports or hobbies would you like to do?

How does the exercise help you? — What should you do to be healthy?

Think about it

How many ways can you think of to encourage people your age to keep fit and healthy?

Writing: A sports information sheet

5 **Read the text. What's in-line skating good for?**

Stay healthy!
Try in-line skating!

In-line skating is great. It's very good aerobic exercise and it builds really strong leg muscles. However, it's not very good for becoming flexible. Skating twice a week for two hours is ideal. It's a brilliant sport for meeting people. You can go skating with a club. It's good fun, too.

You have to be careful because it's easy to pull muscles, so you need to do lots of stretching before and after. And you should wear knee guards and a helmet so that you don't fall and hurt yourself.

6 **Make an information sheet about a sport you like. Find a photo and write about your sport. Use Exercise 5 to help.**

E Revision

1 Find out what household jobs they
have to do. Then write sentences.

1 *Tara has to lay the table.*

2 Complete Sam's blog with the correct form of
(not) have to and *(not) be allowed to*.

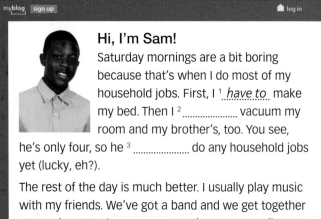

myblog sign up   log in

Hi, I'm Sam!
Saturday mornings are a bit boring
because that's when I do most of my
household jobs. First, I ¹ *have to* make
my bed. Then I ² .... vacuum my
room and my brother's, too. You see,
he's only four, so he ³ .... do any household jobs
yet (lucky, eh?).

The rest of the day is much better. I usually play music
with my friends. We've got a band and we get together
at my place. We ⁴ .... use the garage until 5 p.m.
(Mum says she can't stand the noise later than that!)
Then we go to see a film or eat pizza. I ⁵ .... stay
out too late, though. I ⁶ .... be home by 9.30. I'm
trying to change this – most of my friends ⁷ ....
stay out until 10.30 on Saturdays! No luck, yet!

3 Read Sam's blog again. Ask and answer. Use
have to and *be allowed to*.

1 **A:** *Does Sam have to do household jobs on Saturdays?*
   B: *Yes, he does.*

1 Sam / do household jobs on Saturdays?
2 Sam's brother / vacuum his room?
3 Sam and his friends / play music in the living room?
4 Sam / stay out until 10.00?
5 What time / Sam / be home on Saturdays?
6 Sam's friends / stay out later?

4 Complete the email with the correct form of
have to and the verbs below.

Subject: camping trip   send   save

Hi, Jess,

I'm back from the school camping trip! It was
hard work but great fun! We ¹ *had to carry*
our sleeping bags but we ² .... the tents
because they were already there. We
³ .... early in the morning but I didn't
mind because we did exciting stuff: we went
rock climbing, horse-riding and rafting!

We ⁴ .... dinner most nights but one
evening we made burgers and cooked them on
a real fire. It was fun!

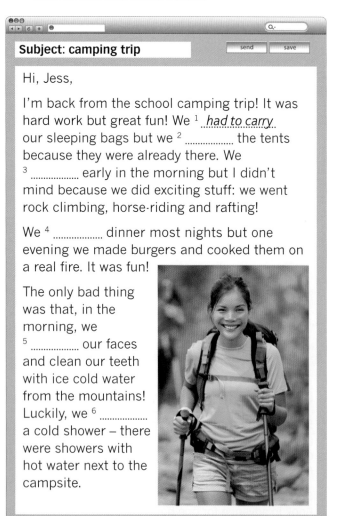

The only bad thing
was that, in the
morning, we
⁵ .... our faces
and clean our teeth
with ice cold water
from the mountains!
Luckily, we ⁶ ....
a cold shower – there
were showers with
hot water next to the
campsite.

| 1 carry ✓ | 3 get up ✓ | 5 wash ✓ |
| 2 carry ✗ | 4 cook ✗ | 6 have ✗ |

5 Match 1–10 with a–j to make phrases.

1 pull a
2 break an
3 have a stomach
4 call an
5 drink lots of
6 put a
7 sprain a
8 cut
9 have sun
10 put an ice

a arm or a leg
b ambulance
c wrist or an ankle
d muscle
e pack on it
f burn
g bug
h water
i bandage on it
j yourself

6 Give advice. Use *should* or *shouldn't* and the phrases in the box.

1 A: *I've got a headache.*
   B: *You should lie down. You shouldn't stay in the sun.*

1 I've got a headache.
2 I've cut my finger.
3 I've sprained my wrist.
4 I think I've broken my leg.
5 I think I've got a stomach bug.
6 I'm really tired!
7 I fainted earlier. I'm still not feeling very well.

call an ambulance	put a plaster on it
eat anything until you feel better	rest
~~lie down~~	stand up too quickly
put an icepack on it	~~stay in the sun~~

7 Complete the dialogue. Then act it out.

Fran: Grandma, I've got a problem. I wore Mum's ring to Tara's party yesterday and I think I've lost it. What ¹ _should_ I do?

Grandma: Why ² .... you ask Tara if she's found it?

Fran: I have! She hasn't found it.

Grandma: I think you ³ .... tell your mum what happened.

Fran: But she'll be angry with me!

Grandma: Well, I think you ⁴ .... apologise. You know you shouldn't take her things without ⁵ ....

Fran: All right but what about the ring?

Grandma: You ⁶ .... buy your mum a new ring.

Fran: But it'll be very expensive!

8 Complete the text with the words in the box.

as	finally	for example	however
~~to begin with~~			

Q: **Some friends and I are travelling around Europe by train this summer. Have you got any advice for us?** *(Andrew, 19)*

A: ¹ _To begin with_ , you should take a backpack, not a suitcase, because it's easier to carry on and off trains. ² ...., make sure it isn't too heavy ³ .... it's tiring to carry a heavy backpack for a long time. You should take something to help pass the time when you're on the train. ⁴ ...., you can read a book or listen to music on your MP3 player. ⁵ ...., make sure you have your mobile with you at all times and call home if there is a problem.

Pronunciation: the silent /l/

9 🔊 2 40 **Listen and repeat.**

My friend Jake ate half a cake
And couldn't go out for a walk.
He filled his mouth as fast
   as he could
And now he can hardly talk!

10 🔊 2 41 **Listen and circle the silent /l/.**

1 wall 2 would 3 should 4 shall 5 old 6 could

My progress

11 **Read and tick (✓).**

I can:	
talk about obligation. *I have to be home by 8.00.*	☐
talk about permission. *I'm allowed to go to bed when I want.*	☐
talk about injuries and illnesses. *I've got a stomach bug.*	☐
give advice about treatment. *You should keep cool.*	☐
give advice. *Why don't you wash it?*	☐

> Turn to Unit 6 Check in the Activity Book on page 72.

pick and mix

How to ...
make friends and stay friends.

Are you a good friend? Read the advice and give yourself a score from 1–5 (1 = I never do this, 5 = I always do this).

1 **Try to be yourself.** You shouldn't try to be someone you aren't. You don't have to be super cool to make good friends. If someone likes you, they'll want to be friends because of *you*, not your clothes or your hairstyle! ☐

2 **Be honest.** You should never lie to your friends. ☐

3 **Keep a secret.** If your friend tells you a secret, do not tell anyone else. You should never talk about your friend behind his/her back. ☐

4 **Do fun things together.** You and your friends should enjoy doing activities and laughing a lot. If you don't have fun then maybe you shouldn't be friends. ☐

5 **You have to look after your friends.** If your friend is in trouble or does something dangerous or silly, you should tell your friend to stop. If they don't stop, you should tell a parent. ☐

6 **Help your friend when he/she is having problems.** Help with homework or listen to him/her if he/she is upset or sad. You should also never laugh at your friend. ☐

7 **Be kind to your friends.** For example, lend them books and DVDs. If you're allowed to borrow your friend's things, you should always give them back. ☐

What's your score? Are you a good friend?

My score = ... / 35

1–10   You'll need to look after your friends if you want to stay friends!

11–24   You're a good friend – but you can always improve a bit!

25–35   You're a great friend! Keep it up!

Quick Quiz
Are you movie mad?

Do the quiz and add up your score to find out.

1 You've seen the film about Willy Wonka, but who wrote the book *Charlie and the Chocolate Factory?*
   a JK Rowling
   b Rudyard Kipling
   c Roald Dahl

2 Who was the director of the fantasy adventure film trilogy *The Lord of The Rings?*
   a Peter Jackson
   b Walt Disney
   c Steven Spielberg

3 Who or what was E.T. in the science fiction film of the same name?
   a a teenage boy
   b a spaceship
   c an alien from a different planet

4 Which title isn't both a book and a film?
   a *The Twilight Saga*
   b *Ice Age*
   c *The Hunger Games*

5 Who does a spider bite in the movie *Spiderman?*
   a Peter Parker
   b Ben Parker
   c Richard Parker

Your score	
More than 4 out of 5	You really know your films! You're movie mad!
Between 2 and 4	OK, you enjoy watching films but you're not mad about them.
Less than 2	You sometimes watch films but you don't know much about them.

STAR SPOT

Complete the text about Chloë Grace Moretz. Use the phrases in the box.

- has sleepovers
- with Johnny Depp
- a small role
- ~~Movie Star under twenty-five~~
- a normal teenager

Chloë Grace Moretz is just a teenager but she has already become a famous actress and she has won at least six awards. In 2012 she won the People's Choice award for Favourite [1] *Movie Star under twenty-five*. She has been an actress since the age of seven, when she had [2] .... as the daughter in *The Amityville Horror* films. But more recently she has starred in comedies like the *Diary of a Wimpy Kid* and the fantasy film *Dark Shadows* [3] ....; the 3D award-winning *Hugo* and the scary horror film *Carrie*. Apart from being an actress, Chloë is just [4] .... She loves shopping, likes social networking and she [5] .... with her friends.
Could *you* be the next Chloë Grace Moretz?

JUST JOKING!

A girl was in hospital with two broken arms and two broken legs. Her friend came to visit. 'What happened?' asked the friend.

'Well, last week I went on a roller coaster. We were coming up to the top of the highest loop when I saw a small sign. I tried to read it but couldn't.

'I was very curious so I went on the roller coaster again. But the roller coaster was so fast I still couldn't read the sign.

'I really wanted to read that sign so I went on the roller coaster a third time. When we got to the top, I stood up in the car to read the sign.'

'And what did it say?' asked her friend.

'Sit down at all times!'

7 More or less

A You must try harder.

Lesson aims:
• say how people do things
• compare how people do things

Presentation

1 🔊 **3 01** **Listen and read. What's happened to Tom's trainers?**

Tara is painting boxes to use in the end-of-year school play. She's asked Dylan and Tom to help her.

Tara: Come on, Dylan! Can't you work faster? We haven't got all day!

Dylan: I'm doing my best!

Tara: Well, try a bit harder!

Tom: Just watch me, Dylan! I'm painting the fastest!

Tara: Yes but you're not painting very carefully! Look! You're dripping paint all over your shoes!

Tom: Oh no! My new trainers!

Dylan: You must be joking! You wore your new trainers to paint in? Maybe I paint more slowly than you do, but at least I've got more brains!

Tom: Says who?

Tara: Guys, stop arguing. Let's make a deal. If we finish earlier than four o'clock, we'll go out for ice cream. My treat.

Tom/Dylan: Done!

2 🔊 **3 02** **Listen and repeat the dialogue.**

English today

• We haven't got all day! • My treat.
• I'm doing my best! • Done!
• Says who?

Comprehension

3 **Read again and complete the sentences with *Tara*, *Dylan* or *Tom*.**

1 *Tara*'s asked for the boys' help.
2 .... isn't working fast.
3 .... paints very fast but he isn't doing a good job.
4 ....'s wearing new trainers.
5 .... wants them to finish before four o'clock.
6 ....'s going to buy ice cream for everyone.

Vocabulary: Adverbs

4 🔊 3 03 **Listen and repeat. Match each adverb with its opposite. Which two words mean the same? Which word doesn't have an opposite?**

badly	carefully	carelessly	early	far
fast	hard	late	loudly	near	quickly
quietly	slowly	well

badly – well

Grammar

Comparative and superlative of adverbs

	Comparative	Superlative
quickly	**more** quickly	**the** quick**est**
slowly	**more** slowly	**the** slow**est**
hard	hard**er**	**the** hard**est**
late	lat**er**	**the** lat**est**
fast	fast**er**	**the** fast**est**
well	better	**the** best
badly	worse	**the** worst
far	further	**the** furthest

5 **Look at the pictures and write sentences.**

1 *Kieran is playing the guitar badly but David is playing worse.*

| 1 play guitar / badly | 3 eat / slowly |
| 2 arrive at school / late | 4 dance / well |

6 **Look at the table and write sentences.**

1 *Tom works harder than Dylan but Tara works the hardest.*

	Dylan	Tara	Tom
1 Work hard at school	67%	92%	78%
2 Do well at sports	****	***	**
3 Run fast (short distance)	6 miles per hour	8 miles per hour	4 miles per hour
4 Go to bed late	11.30 p.m.	9.30 p.m.	10.00 p.m.
5 Get up early	8.15 a.m.	7.15 a.m.	7.00 a.m.
6 Cycle far	10 miles	7 miles	8 miles

Speaking

7 **A: Imagine you're B's teacher. Make comments (1–6). B: Respond using a–f.**

1 A: *You're speaking too loudly.*
   B: *Sorry, I'll speak more quietly.*

1 You're speaking too loudly.
2 You didn't read the question carefully.
3 You didn't do well in the last History test.
4 You're reading too fast.
5 You're very late with your project.
6 You're working too noisily!

a I'm sorry. I / try / hard next time
b ~~Sorry, I / speak / quietly~~
c I'm sorry. I / finish / it / early next time
d OK, I / read / slowly
e Sorry, we / work / quietly
f OK, I / read it / carefully

8 **Student A: go to page 103.**
   Student B: go to page 107.

About you

9 **Ask and answer about your friends.**

1 A: *Which of your friends runs faster than you?*
   B: *Marina runs faster than I do.*
   A: *Which of your friends runs the fastest?*
   B: *I think Olivia runs the fastest.*

1 run fast	4 cycle far
2 go to bed late	5 live near the city centre
3 get up early	

> Now turn to Unit 7A in the Activity Book.

B The least stressful way ...

Lesson aims:
• compare buildings
• write about an interesting building

London's Biggest and Best
by Tom Harper

Here are two of the most AMAZING buildings in London.

This is the Shard. Why is it called that? It's a skyscraper that looks like a piece of broken glass. It's the tallest building in Europe, with a height of ¹ _310_ metres. The view from the ² .... floor is spectacular. Inside there are restaurants, offices, a hotel and flats. It's a vertical city!

My opinion:
It's a great tourist attraction but the entrance tickets, which cost ³ ...., should be less expensive. The cheapest way to visit the Shard is to book tickets online in advance. This is the easiest and least stressful way, too.

This building is called the Gherkin – can you guess why? It isn't as popular with tourists as the Shard because it's just an office building. But it's cool to look at. There are no walls but lots of windows – ⁴ .... square metres of glass! It's the ⁵ .... tallest building in London. It has ⁶ .... floors and if you walk to the top you'll have to climb ⁷ .... stairs!

My opinion:
It isn't as tall as the Shard but it's just as impressive.

Presentation

1 (3 04) **Listen and read. Complete the text with the numbers in the box.**

~~310~~	72nd	1,037	6th	24,000	£24.95	38

Comprehension

2 **Read again and answer *True* (T), *False* (F) or *Doesn't say* (DS).**

1 The view from the Shard is the one of the best in London. ☐ _T_
2 There are only offices inside the Shard. ☐
3 You can visit the Shard. ☐
4 Over 100 families live inside the Shard. ☐
5 There's a hotel inside the Gherkin. ☐
6 The Gherkin is 180 metres tall. ☐
7 The Gherkin is the tallest building in London. ☐

Vocabulary: Buildings and parts of buildings

3 (3 05) **Listen and repeat. Label the words *Building* (B) or *Part of building* (P).**

block of flats *B*   ceiling   door   flat
(ground, first, second, top) floor   house   office
palace   roof   room   skyscraper   stairs
theatre   wall   window

4 **Describe your school building. Use the words in Exercise 3.**

My school is quite big. It's got three floors and it's got a small theatre. The classrooms are on the first and second floors and there are offices on the top floor. The rooms all have big windows.

Grammar

Comparatives: *(not) as … as, less … than*
It's **(just) as impressive as** the Shard.
It is**n't as tall as** the Shard.
The tickets should be **less expensive than** they are.

Superlative: *the least*
It's **the least stressful** way to visit the Shard.

About you

5 Give your opinion by making comparisons. Use the adjectives in the box.

| boring | dangerous | difficult | exciting | fun |
| healthy | tasty | | | |

1 cats / dogs / parrots
I think that cats are as much fun as dogs. Parrots are the least fun.
2 skateboarding / roller skating / cycling
3 chocolate ice cream / yoghurt / banana milkshakes
4 skiing holidays / beach holidays / camping holidays

6 Ask and answer about the buildings.

A: *Which building took the least time to build?*
B: *The Empire State Building in New York took the least time to build. It only took a year and a half!*

Which building …
• took the least time / longest to build?
• is the tallest / the least tall?
• has the highest number / the lowest number of floors?
• is the most / the least popular?

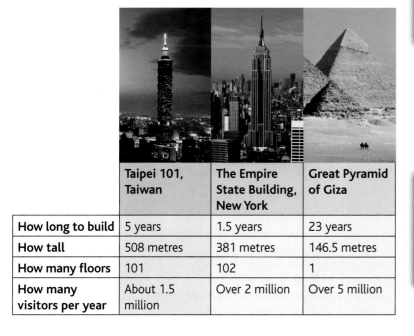

	Taipei 101, Taiwan	The Empire State Building, New York	Great Pyramid of Giza
How long to build	5 years	1.5 years	23 years
How tall	508 metres	381 metres	146.5 metres
How many floors	101	102	1
How many visitors per year	About 1.5 million	Over 2 million	Over 5 million

Listening

7 **3 06** Listen to a guided tour of Shakespeare's Globe Theatre and complete the text.

The Globe Theatre, London

Shakepeare's Globe Theatre – past and present

I Richard Burbage built the first Globe Theatre in [1] *1599*. It was [2] .... high and 3,000 people could watch the plays there. Today only [3] .... people fit in Shakespeare's Globe.

II In 1613 the theatre burnt down. It had a straw [4] .... and a special effect on stage started the fire.

III In the sixteenth century, [5] .... didn't use to act in the theatre. They weren't allowed.

IV The theatre was as [6] .... and as expensive then as it is today. People used to come from all around to enjoy the day.

Writing

8 Think of an interesting building in your country. Compare it to the Gherkin or the Shard.

The Colosseum is one of the most popular tourist attractions in Rome. It's older than the Shard. It's nearly two thousand years old! But it's just as interesting as the Shard.

> Now turn to Unit 7B in the Activity Book.

C Lots of monkeys ...

Presentation

1 Listen and read. Choose the correct words.

To: madbrad@connectmail.co.uk   send   save

From: dyljones13@ukonline.com

Subject: Woburn Safari Park

Hi Bradley,

I've just been to Woburn Safari Park. It's only about an hour from Cambridge. You ¹*have to* / *shouldn't* go!

The ²*best* / *worst* bit was the monkey enclosure. Lots of monkeys jumped on the car. I think they were ³*angry* / *hungry*. Tara had a little bread in her hand and they took it! She opened her window – big mistake!

The zebras and the giraffes were ⁴*funny* / *beautiful*. But we couldn't get very close because there were too many ⁵*people* / *children* around.

The penguins were cute but they weren't much fun. They just made a lot of noise and they can't fly! ⁶*And* / *However*, the camels were awesome. Their humps make them look really different. There aren't many animals as ⁷*ugly* / *beautiful* as they are!

We saw one or two rhinos, too (those horns are scary!) but we didn't see many 'big cats' – only a few lions (did you know that lions are the only cats with manes?). I think the tigers were ⁸*sleeping* / *eating*.

Unfortunately, we didn't have enough time to see the lemurs. They come out at night. One day just isn't enough to visit Woburn!

Why don't you go for your birthday next month?

Dylan

Comprehension

2 Read again and answer the questions.

1 How far from Cambridge is Woburn?
2 What was Dylan's favourite part of Woburn?
3 Why didn't they get close to the giraffes and zebras?
4 Which animal is very ugly?
5 Which animal was a bit boring?
6 What were the tigers doing?
7 Did Dylan visit everything?
8 When should Bradley visit Woburn?

Vocabulary: Wild animals

3 Listen and repeat. Which animals are in Dylan's photos?

| camel | cheetah | giraffe | lemur | lion | monkey |
| penguin | rhinoceros (rhino) | tiger | zebra |

monkey

4 Which animals in Exercise 3 ...

1 are part of the cat family?
   cheetahs ... ,
2 are birds but don't fly?
3 have **a** humps **b** horns?
4 mostly eat meat or fish?
5 mostly eat plants, vegetables or insects?
6 mostly live in trees?

Grammar

Quantifiers

Countable nouns

A lot of/Lots of monkeys jumped on the car.

We saw a tiger and **a few** lions.

We saw **one or two** rhinos.

There **aren't many** animals as ugly as they are!

Uncountable nouns

We had **a lot of/lots of** fun

Tara had **a little** bread in her hand.

They were**n't much** fun.

There were **too many** people around.

We didn't have **enough** time to see the lemurs.

5 **Choose the correct words.**

1 There were *a lot of* / *a little* monkeys.

2 There were *too much* / *too many* people.

3 There wasn't *enough* / *too much* time to see everything.

4 There were only *one or two* / *many* big cats.

5 Dylan saw *a little* / *a few* rhinos.

6 The penguins made *many* / *a lot of* noise.

6 **Complete the text with the words in the box.**

a few	a little	lot of	many	many
~~much~~	too many	too much	two	

They bought a zoo – it's true!

When Benjamin Mee and his family bought a zoo in England in 1997, they didn't have [1] *much* money and they only had [2] .... experience.

There weren't [3] .... people who wanted to buy the zoo because there were too [4] .... animals. The zoo had just [5] .... lions and one or [6] ...., tigers but it had a [7] .... monkeys. The animals needed [8] .... food and the zoo needed [9] .... hours of work but Benjamin and his family worked hard and today you can visit over 200 animals in Dartmoor Zoo. It's a great day out!

Benjamin Mee at Dartmoor Zoo

Speaking

7 **Read the review of Lenthorpe Wildlife Park. Ask and answer.**

1 A: *Is it big?*

B: *Yes, it is. There are 4,000 square metres of park and there are a lot of play areas.*

> **TRIP TIPS** **Lenthorpe Wildlife Park**
>
> ✓ 4,000 square metres of park with five play areas
> ✓ One of the widest varieties of big cats in the UK (tigers, lions, cheetahs) and many more animals
> ✓ Small numbers of visitors
> ✓ Cheap entrance tickets (£4)
> ✗ A few of the animals' cages were a bit small and dirty
> ✗ Only one café (take a picnic!)
> ✗ Couldn't find much information about the animals

1 Is it big?

2 Are there any interesting animals?

3 Is it busy?

4 Are tickets expensive?

5 Are all the animals clean and happy?

6 Are there any cafés or restaurants?

7 Can you learn a lot about the animals?

Writing

8 **Imagine you visited Lenthorpe Wildlife Park. Write about it in an email to a friend. Write one paragraph about the good things and one paragraph about the bad things.**

> **Subject: Lenthorpe Wildlife Park** send save
>
> Dear Molly,
> Lenthorpe Wildlife Park was good fun but it wasn't brilliant.
> ....
> ....
> See you soon.
> Love,
> ....

> Now turn to Unit 7C in the Activity Book.

D Communication

Speaking: Ask for and give recommendations

1 DVD (3/09) **Listen and read.** *Mr and Mrs Woods are visiting Cambridge for the first time. They ask Tara and Dylan for some information.*

1

Mr Woods: Excuse me, do you live around here?

Dylan: Yes, we do. Can we help you?

Mrs Woods: We're looking for somewhere to have lunch with our grandsons. Can you recommend a good restaurant?

Dylan: You could try 'Burger Stop'. It's round the corner.

2

Tara: I think you'll like 'Salt & Pepper' better. It's a bit further away from here but it's very good.

Dylan: But 'Burger Stop' is much better value! You can eat as many burgers as you want for £8.

Tara: Yes but there isn't much choice on their menu. They've only got burgers!

3

Tara: There are lots of different things on the menu at 'Salt & Pepper'.

Mr Woods: Well, thank you very much. You've been very helpful.

Mrs Woods: I think we'll try 'Salt & Pepper'. It sounds really nice.

2 (3/10) **Complete the dialogue. Choose a or b. Then listen and check.**

Man: Excuse me, ¹ *do you live around here* ?

Fran: Yes, we do. Can we help?

Woman: We'd like to do some sightseeing. ² ....

Tom: You could try the University Museum of Zoology. It's round the corner.

Fran: I think ³ .... the Fitzwilliam Museum better.

Tom: But the Zoology Museum is great if you love animals.

Fran: Yes but ⁴ .... the Fitzwilliam Museum.

Man: Well, thank you very much. ⁵ ....

Woman: I think we'll try the Fitzwilliam Museum.

1 **a** do you live around here **b** can we ask you a question
2 **a** Where can we stay? **b** Can you recommend a museum?
3 **a** you won't like **b** you'll like
4 **a** it isn't as nice as **b** it's a lot better
5 **a** You've been very helpful. **b** You'll be very helpful.

English today

- Can you recommend (a good restaurant)?
- You could try ('Burger Stop').
- I think you'll like ('Salt & Pepper') better.
- You've been very helpful.

Your turn

3 **A: Imagine you're visiting a town for the first time. Ask B and C to recommend:**

- a place where you can have a cup of coffee.
- any interesting places to see.
- a place where you can buy some local food.

Use Exercise 2 to help you write a dialogue. Then act it out.

Writing: A guide to my town

4 Read the guide to Cambridge and match the headings (a–c) with the paragraphs (1–3).

a Eating and drinking   **b** Shopping   **c** Culture and fun

Come to Cambridge!

......

1 There are lots of interesting things to do in Cambridge. Besides visiting the famous university colleges, you can go to museums as well as the theatre or a live concert. There are other fun things you can do, too. You can hire a bike or go on a ghost tour! You can also hire a punt (a type of rowing boat) and go rowing down the river Cam.

......

2 In addition to the variety of shops in the town there are two new shopping centres. Don't forget to have a look at our busy outdoor market, too. You'll find everything there – from books, jewellery and hats to local fresh fruit and vegetables.

......

3 However, you won't be able to do all your shopping and sightseeing if you don't eat! Cambridge offers a wide choice of cafés and restaurants. You'll find some of the best restaurants here. You'll also find lots of very good value restaurants where you can have a tasty meal without spending a lot.

Punting on the River Cam

Writing tip

Adverbs and adverbial phrases of addition

When you want to add more to what you've already said, you can use an adverb or adverbial phrase of addition.

Look at the text in Exercise 4 and circle these adverbs/ adverbial phrases.

also   as well as   besides   in addition to   too

5 Choose the correct words to complete the brochure.

Welcome to our town!

There are lots of things to do in our town. You can visit the ruins of the ancient market and the archaeological museum next to it. There's [1] *too* / *also* an ancient theatre near the city centre.

[2] *Also* / *Besides* sightseeing, the city centre is the place to go shopping. You'll find all the latest fashions [3] *as well as* / *too* local products like our famous cheese.

[4] *In addition to* / *Also* the shops in the centre, there is an outdoor market by the river every Saturday where you can find old books and antiques. If you go there, don't forget to have a glass of fresh lemonade, [5] *besides* / *too*. It's the best, and it's from the local lemon trees!

Your turn

6 In groups, write a short guide to your town or city. Use Exercises 4 and 5 to help.

What should a visitor to your town do? Write about these topics. Use adverbs and adverbial phrases of addition.

- Student A: Culture and fun
- Student B: Shopping
- Student C: Eating and drinking

There are lots of things to do in our town. You can visit ... and ... . There's also ... . Besides sightseeing, the city centre is ... .

> Now turn to page 85 in the Activity Book.

The British and their love of animals

The British love animals. More than 50 percent of British families have pets. They have eight million cats, one million birds, like budgies or parrots, and forty million fish. The most popular fish are goldfish and tropical fish. They also keep small farm animals and snakes and other reptiles as well. But it doesn't end there …

Pets in Britain   millions

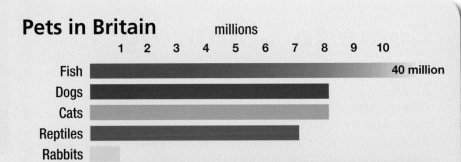

	1	2	3	4	5	6	7	8	9	10
Fish										40 million
Dogs										
Cats										
Reptiles										
Rabbits										
Birds										
Guinea pigs										
Hamsters										
Chickens, etc.										
Frogs/Toads										
Horses/Ponies										

Nature programmes

The British enjoy watching nature programmes, too. They especially love the British naturalist David Attenborough. He's one of the best-known presenters of nature documentaries on TV. Not many people have visited as many places or observed as many wild animals as he has. He has travelled to some of the coldest, hottest, wettest and wildest places on the planet. His amazing documentaries have taught people a lot about rare and wild animals on TV.

FACT: In the UK, 40 percent of people watch nature programmes every week.

Volunteering

I'm sixteen now so I'm volunteering at an animal rescue centre. It's brilliant. I have to work harder than my friends in other part-time jobs but I'm learning so much about animal care. I help to feed the animals and clean out the cages. Yesterday I had to feed a baby monkey with a tiny spoon. I've never done anything as exciting as that before!

Sally, 16

FACT: The UK was the first country to make a law to protect animals.

New words

budgie (budgerigar)   cage   (animal) care   law
naturalist   nature   observe   rare   reptile

Reading

1 🎧 3/11 Listen and read. Who is David Attenborough?

Comprehension

2 Read again and complete the fact file.

Quick facts

- At least [1] *50 percent* of British families have a pet.
- The most popular pets are [2] ....·
- The least popular pets are [3] ....·
- British people really love watching [4] .... on TV. Many people watch them [5] ....·
- From the age of [6] .... British teenagers can volunteer in animal rescue centres.
- The UK was the [7] .... country to fight for animal rights.

Listening

3 🎧 3/12 Listen and answer *True* (*T*) or *False* (*F*).

Termite

Beaver

1 Brooke has already seen the documentary *Animal House*. ⬚F⬚

2 Brooke enjoyed the programme *Frozen Planet*. ⬚

3 *Animal House* is a programme about people's homes. ⬚

4 A termite home is like a skyscraper. ⬚

5 *Animal House* is on TV every day. ⬚

6 Beavers have teeth that grow very fast. ⬚

Think about it

A pet can make people happier, healthier, fitter and less stressed. Do you agree?

Speaking

4 Ask and answer about animals in your country.

1 **A:** *What pet do you have or would you like to have?*
   B: *I haven't got a pet but I'd like to have a dog.*
   A: *Why?*
   B: *Because there are lots of parks near my house. You can walk a dog in the park and dogs are fun.*

1 What pet do you have or would you like to have?

2 Do you enjoy watching nature programmes? What programmes have you seen?

3 What zoos or wildlife parks have you visited? Which was your favourite?

4 Which wild animal do you think is the most interesting/the least interesting? Why?

Project: An amazing animal

5 Read about the polar bear. Which fact is the most interesting to you?

An amazing animal: the polar bear

The polar bear is the largest bear in the world. Some males can be three metres tall and can weigh as much as 700 kilos. They live mostly in the Arctic, where the temperature can go down to -45 degrees.

Polar bears keep warm because they have thick fur, small ears and short tails. They eat seals and fish. They find food easily because they can smell a seal under the ice from many kilometres away. Unfortunately, there aren't many polar bears left – only about 22,000 in the world.

Interesting fact: Polar bear fur isn't white. It doesn't have any colour! The white colour comes from snow and light.

6 Write about a wild animal. Find a photo and include at least one interesting fact.

The elephant: the largest land animal

Elephants are the largest land animals in the world. Their trunks can be up to two metres long and can weigh as much as 140 kilos.

Interesting fact: An elephant uses its trunk like a snorkel to help it swim underwater.

F Revision

1 **Match the sentences (1–4) with the pictures (A–D).**

1 Can you speak more loudly, please? `C`
2 Can't you walk faster? We're late! ☐
3 Please play your music more quietly. I've got a terrible headache. ☐
4 I'm busy right now. Can you call back later? ☐

A

B

C

D

2 **Match the descriptions (1–9) with the words (a–i).**

1 A lot of people have their homes in this building. `b`
2 The Gherkin has thirty-eight of these. ☐
3 a very tall building ☐
4 You look out of a room through this. ☐
5 You walk into a room through this. ☐
6 People usually work here. ☐
7 These are usually inside a building. You have to climb them to get higher. ☐
8 This is above your head in a room. ☐
9 This stops the rain coming into a building. ☐

a a roof	**d** stairs	**g** a skyscraper
b a block of flats	**e** a window	**h** an office
c a door	**f** floors	**i** a ceiling

3 **Look at the table. Compare the adventure parks.**

1 **A:** *Aqua World is as expensive as Escape Land.*
  B: *Heaton Towers is less expensive than Aqua World.*
  C: *Heaton Towers is the least expensive of the three.*

1 Tickets: expensive
2 Rides: exciting
3 Visitors: popular
4 Restaurants: good

	Aqua World	Heaton Towers	Escape Land
1 Day ticket	£25	£20	£25
2 Rides	*****	*****	**
3 Visitors	2.2 million per year	2.2 million per year	800,000 per year
4 Restaurants	****	**	****

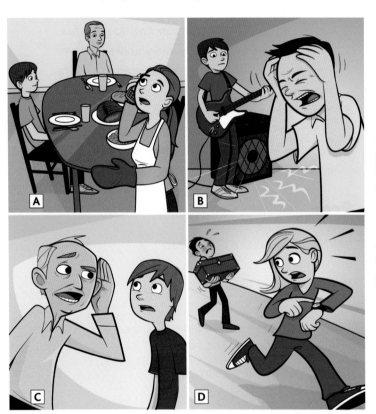

4 **Which animal am I? Match the words in the box with the sentences.**

camel	~~cheetah~~	giraffe	lemur	lion
monkey	penguin	rhino	tiger	zebra

1 I run the fastest. I'm from the cat family. *cheetah*
2 I've got black and white stripes. ....
3 I like to swim and I eat a lot of fish, too. ....
4 I use my long arms to move from tree to tree. ....
5 I'm not a monkey but I live in the trees, too. I come out at night. ....
6 I have a big horn on my nose. ....
7 I have humps on my back. ....
8 I'm from the cat family, too. I'm the only cat with a mane. ....
9 I'm very tall and I've got a long neck. I eat the leaves from trees. ....
10 I'm also from the cat family. I've got stripes. ....

5 Complete the text with the words in the box.

few	little	a lot of	~~lots~~	many	much
one	too				

myblog sign up   log in

We visited Aqua World last weekend. The tickets were expensive (there were four of us) but they were good value because we had ¹ _lots_ of fun! My little brother couldn't go on a ² .... of the rides because he wasn't old enough but I went everywhere. There were ³ .... or two rides I didn't like but the others were brilliant! I liked the 'Space Rocket' the most. The good thing was that there weren't ⁴ .... people in the queue so I went twice!

We had lunch at one of the restaurants but there wasn't ⁵ .... choice on their menu: they only had sandwiches and burgers. In the end, we sat on the grass and had a picnic because there were ⁶ .... many people in the restaurant and we couldn't find a table. I wasn't very hungry so I just had a ⁷ .... bread and a packet of crisps. However, I took ⁸ .... photos as you can see! I hope we can go again soon!

6 Put the dialogue in the correct order. Then act it out.

☐ **Tara:** You could try 'Brown's'. It's round the corner.

☐ **Man:** Well, thank you very much. You've been very helpful. I think I'll try 'Shop One'. It sounds really good.

☐ **Man:** I'm looking for somewhere to buy a shirt. Can you recommend a shop?

☐ **Tara:** But 'Brown's' is much better value. The prices are really low!

☐ **Tom:** Yes, we do. Can we help you?

☐ **Tom:** I think you'll like 'Shop One' better. It's a bit further away from here but it's very good.

[1] **Man:** Excuse me do you live around here?

☐ **Tom:** Yes, but there isn't much choice. They've got very few styles! There's lots of choice at 'Shop One'.

7 Choose the correct words.

There are lots of interesting things to do in London. ¹ (Besides)/ Also visiting the famous sights, you can visit museums and galleries, the world famous London Zoo or the London Aquarium.

I know you're a great footballer but there are lots of other sports you can try ² also / as well as football.

There's a big choice of cafés and restaurants in our area. They serve British food but you can ³ in addition to / also find lots of Chinese and Indian restaurants.

Can I have a chicken salad and a ham sandwich, ⁴ too / besides?

Pronunciation: the schwa /ə/

8 (3 13) Listen and repeat.
Look **at** my beautiful castle,
It's bigg**er** **and** bett**er** than yours.
It took me ov**er** **an** hour t**o** make
But **at** least it's got windows **and** doors!

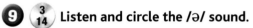

9 (3 14) Listen and circle the /ə/ sound.
1 Their gard(e)n looks prettier than ours.
2 My kitchen isn't as big as yours.
3 I can run faster than my father.
4 Tina has a better answer for the second question.

My progress

10 Read and tick (✓).

I can:	
say how people do things. *She speaks very loudly.*	☐
compare how people do things. *Dylan paints more slowly than Tom.*	☐
compare buildings. *This flat is less expensive than that one.*	☐
talk about wild animals. *We saw one or two rhinos.*	☐
talk about quantities. *Tara had a little bread in her hand.*	☐
ask for and give recommendations. *You could try 'Burger Stop'.*	☐

> Turn to Unit 7 Check in the Activity Book on page 86.

8 Our world

A Plastic is recycled, too.

Lesson aims:
• identify materials and containers
• describe processes

Presentation

1 (3/15) **Listen and read.**

What does Tom say about recycling?

Dylan: Right, we have to put the rubbish in the correct bins. Paper, cardboard, tins and glass are all recycled so they go in the blue bin.

Tom: What about plastic?

Dylan: Plastic is recycled too but only bottles and pots.

Tom: What are the green bins for?

Dylan: Food waste. And the green bag is for garden waste. Food and garden waste is composted. And anything that isn't recycled goes in the black bin. Plastic carrier bags or crisp packets – stuff like that.

Tom: Is the rubbish collected every week?

Dylan: Well, one week the blue and green bins are collected and the next week the black bin. By the way, thanks for helping. I hate sorting rubbish!

Tom: Yes but recycling is good for the environment. It saves energy and reduces pollution.

Dylan: Hey, did you know some fleece jumpers are made from recycled plastic bottles?

Tom: Yuk! No wonder my fleece smells funny!

2 (3/16) **Listen and repeat the dialogue.**

English today

• Right, ...
• ... stuff like that
• By the way, ...
• Thanks for helping.
• No wonder (my fleece smells funny).

Comprehension

3 **Read again and choose the correct answers.**

1 The Jones' rubbish goes inside ...
   a one bin. **b** several bins.

2 Plastic bottles go in the ...
   a blue bin. **b** green bin.

3 The green bins are for ...
   a food waste. **b** paper.

4 Someone collects rubbish for recycling ...
   a every week. **b** twice a month.

5 In Cambridge, they don't recycle ...
   a plastic carrier bags. **b** plastic pots.

6 Dylan thinks sorting rubbish is ...
   a an OK job. **b** an awful job.

Vocabulary: Containers and materials

4 🎧 3/17 Listen and repeat. Label the words *Container* (**C**) or *Material* (**M**). Which two words can be both?

aluminium (can) *M*   (carrier) bag *C*   bin bottle   box   can (of cola)   cardboard (juice/milk) carton   glass   jar packet (of biscuits/crisps)   paper   plastic (yoghurt) pot   steel   tin (of baked beans)

5 Look at the photo on page 88 again. What objects and materials can you see?

plastic rubbish bins

6 Look at the pictures and read the sentences. Complete the sentences with the present simple passive. Then number the pictures in the correct order.

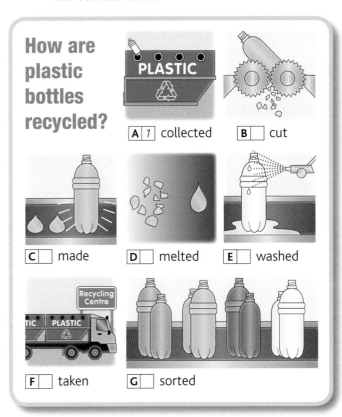

How are plastic bottles recycled?

PLASTIC

[A] [1] collected   [B] [ ] cut
[C] [ ] made   [D] [ ] melted   [E] [ ] washed

Recycling Centre

PLASTIC

[F] [ ] taken   [G] [ ] sorted

1 The bottles __are collected__ in bottle banks.
2 They .... to the Recycling Centre.
3 First, the bottles ....·
4 Then, they .... into colours.
5 Next, they .... into small pieces of plastic.
6 The pieces of plastic ....·
7 Finally, the melted plastic .... into new things.

Grammar

Present simple passive:
be + past participle

Positive and negative

Paper	**is**	**recycled.**
Garden waste	**is**	**composted.**
Some fleece jumpers	**are**	**made** from recycled plastic bottles.
Some waste	**isn't**	**recycled.**
Carrier bags	**aren't**	**recycled.**

Questions

Is the rubbish **collected** every week?
How are plastic bottles **recycled**?

Speaking

7 Look at Exercise 6 again. Explain to your partner how plastic bottles are recycled.

The bottles are collected in bottle banks. ...

8 Student A: go to page 103.
Student B: go to page 107.

Listening

9 🎧 3/18 Listen and complete the answers.

Plastic fantastic Melissa shoes

1 What are Melissa shoes made of?   ..*plastic*..
2 What's special about this material? It gets ....
   when it's warm.
3 Where are Melissa shoes made?   in ....
4 How are Melissa shoes different? They're eco-...............·
5 How much of its waste does the   .... percent
   factory recycle?
6 What do Melissa shoes smell like? ....

About you

10 Ask and answer with your partner.

1 What things does your family recycle? Make a list.
2 What waste is collected from your home? What do you have to take to a recycling centre?

> Now turn to Unit 8A in the Activity Book.

B It was called smellovision!

Lesson aims:
- express opinions and describe feelings
- report past events

The (Hoax) Museum
Smellovision

Here's an amusing true story about the power of TV. In 1965, a professor from London University was invited by the BBC to appear on TV. He was interviewed about his new invention. It was called smellovision and it could send smells from the TV studio into people's homes.

To show how this worked, the professor put some coffee beans and then some onions into the smellovision machine. Viewers were asked to stand about two metres from their TV sets, sniff and phone the studio if they smelled anything.

People from around the country phoned and said, 'We can really smell coffee and onions!' They were very excited. Some even said, 'The onions made my eyes water!'

The TV people were surprised. Why? Because the programme was a hoax! The technology didn't exist! The viewers couldn't really smell these things at all!

We may find this funny and embarrassing now but fifty years ago TV was a new and exciting technology. Most people didn't understand how it worked and they were ready to believe anything!

Presentation

1 🔊 3 19 **Listen and read. Can you guess what hoax means?**

Comprehension

2 **Read again and write True (T), False (F) or Doesn't say (DS).**

1 The professor talked about his invention on BBC radio. [F]

2 He was a science professor at London University. ☐

3 The professor said smellovision used people's TV sets to send smells into their homes. ☐

4 The professor put some coffee and some onions into a TV set. ☐

5 More than one thousand viewers called the studio that day. ☐

6 Some viewers cried because they smelled onions. ☐

7 Fifty years ago very few people had a TV. ☐

Vocabulary: Adjectives with -ed/-ing endings

3 🔊 3 20 **Listen and repeat. Tick (✓) the adjectives with a positive meaning and cross (✗) the ones with a negative meaning. Which adjectives can have both meanings?**

Someone/something is ...	You are/feel ...	Someone/something is ...	You are/feel ...
amusing	amused ✓	exciting	excited ☐
annoying	annoyed ☐	frightening	frightened ☐
boring	bored ☐	interesting	interested ☐
embarrassing	embarrassed ☐	surprising	surprised ☐

4 **Ask and answer.**

1 **A:** *What's the most exciting thing you've ever done?*
   B: *I went white-water rafting last summer.*

1 What's the most exciting thing you've ever done?
2 What's the most annoying thing someone has done to you?
3 What's the most interesting book you've ever read?
4 What's the most frightening film you've ever watched?
5 What's the most amusing thing you've ever heard?

5 **Complete the sentences. Then tell the class.**

1 I feel excited when *I go on holiday with my family* .
2 I feel annoyed when ... .   4 I feel bored when ... .
3 I feel surprised when ... .   5 I feel embarrassed when ... .

Grammar

Past simple passive: *be* + past participle

Positive and negative

The professor **was** interviewed on TV.
The professor **wasn't** interviewed on the radio.

be* + past participle + *by

The professor **was** invited **by** the BBC.

Questions

What were the viewers **asked** to do?
Who was the professor **invited** by?

6 **Write the questions. Then ask and answer about the story in Exercise 1. Use the past simple passive.**

1 **A:** *What was the new invention called?*
B: *It was called smellovision.*

1 What / the new invention / call?
2 Who / it / invent by?
3 Where / the professor / interview?
4 Who / he / invite by?
5 What / put / into / the smellovision machine?
6 What / the viewers / ask / to do?

7 **Finish the story. Use the questions to help.**

1 Who was surprised?
2 Why were they surprised?
3 Why did viewers believe the hoax?

8 **Complete the texts with the correct forms of the verbs. One is a hoax, the other is true. Which is which?**

Writing

9 **Complete the text about an Internet hoax. Use the information below and the past simple passive.**

How to charge an iPod:

- Pour two cups of an energy drink into a jug.
- Make some holes in an onion.
- Place the onion in the jug.
- Leave it there for thirty minutes.
- Then take the onion out of the jug.
- Dry it with a towel.
- Push the iPod charger into the onion.
- Connect the charger to the iPod.

Can an onion really charge an iPod?

One of the funniest Internet hoaxes ever was a video that showed how to charge an iPod using just an onion and an energy drink. This is how it was done:

Two cups of an energy drink were poured into a jug. ...

In the video, the iPod started to charge!

Unfortunately, lots of people believed it and tried it at home. But they were only left with an iPod that smelled of onions!

Now turn to Unit 8B in the Activity Book.

20th February 2013: A forty-year-old ¹ was saved (save) by a six-year-old.

Frank Dane, forty-two, from Sussex fainted while he was driving his car. Six-year-old Elsie, who was sitting next to him, grabbed the wheel and managed to stop the car. Frank ² .... (take) to hospital and is now well. Unfortunately Elsie ³ .... (not interview) by our reporters. Why? Because she can't speak – Elsie is a chimp!

4th June 2011: A not very Happy Birthday!

A birthday party invitation ⁴ .... (post) by a German girl on a social networking site. She ⁵ .... (call) Thessa and she only wanted to invite her friends. However, it ⁶ .... (not mark) 'private' so 1,500 people arrived at her house!

C Communication

Speaking: Say goodbye

1   **Listen and read.** *Tom is going back home to Chicago. Dylan and his dad are taking him to the airport.*

1

Tom: Goodbye, Mrs Jones and thank you for everything.

Mum: Bye, Tom. We've enjoyed having you here. Give my regards to your mum and dad.

Tom: I will. And I'll tell them how well you looked after me.

Mum: Oh, that's nice. Please come and see us again!

Tom: I'd love to.

2

Tom: Bye, Tara. Look after yourself.

Tara: You, too. We're going to miss you.

Tom: Good luck with the singing.

Tara: Thanks, Tom. Have a good journey and don't forget to keep in touch, OK?

Tom: I won't, I promise.

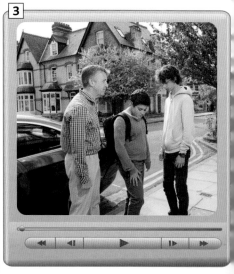

3

Dad: We should go. Have you got your passport, Tom?

Tom: Yes, it's in my rucksack with my ticket.

Dylan: Have you got the medal you were given by the rugby team?

Tom: It should be in my pocket. Yes, it's right here.

Dad: Great, let's go.

2 **3 22** **Complete the dialogue. Use the English today box. Then listen and check.**

Lisa: Goodbye, Mrs Gordon. [1] *Thank you for everything* .

Mrs Gordon: Bye, Lisa. It's been lovely having you here. [2] ....

Lisa: Me, too.

Mrs Gordon: Don't forget, [3] ....

Lisa: I will. I'll tell them what a brilliant time I've had.

Mrs Gordon: Oh, that's nice. [4] ....

Lisa: [5] .... Maybe next year.

Mrs Gordon: Yes, that's a good idea. Now, [6] ....

Lisa: There'll be lots of films to watch on the plane so no problem.

Mrs Gordon: Great. Bye, [7] ....

Lisa: Yes, I'll email when I arrive.

English today

- Thank you (for everything).
- Give my regards to your mum and dad.
- Please come and see us again!
- I'd love to.
- I'm/We're going to miss you.
- Have a good flight/journey.
- Keep in touch.

Your turn

3 **A:** You're saying goodbye to your host family.
B: You're the son or daughter in the host family.
Use Exercise 2 to help you write a dialogue.
Then act it out.

A: Goodbye, ... Thank you for everything.
B: Bye, ... I'm going to miss you ...

Writing: A thank you letter

4 Read Tom's letter and answer *True* (*T*) or *False* (*F*). Correct the false sentences.

1 Tom liked visiting London best of all. ☐
2 Everyone at Tom's school plays rugby. ☐
3 Dylan's family are invited to Chicago. ☐

Dear All,

I'm writing to say thank you very much for having me to stay. I had a really great time in cambridge.

I've told Mum and Dad all about it. It was great fun when we went sightseeing in London. That old prison, The Clink, was scary! And I realy enjoyed our camping trip to the Lake District. It's a beautiful place. Best of all, I learnt to play rugby with Dylan. I'm the only person at my school who can play it.

Mum and Dad say please come to Chicago and visit us. Why don't you come next summer.

Once again a big, big thank you!

Best wishes,

Tom

P.S. Dylan, dont forget to email me that photo! You know, the one you took when I was given my rugby medal!

Writing tip

Writing a thank you letter

Paragraphing

Divide your letter into paragraphs.

Punctuation

Check your spelling and punctuation. Use capital letters correctly.

Language

Make sure you are polite.

Look at Tom's letter again and answer the questions.

How many paragraphs are there? What does each paragraph do?

Find one example of polite language.

There are four punctuation/spelling mistakes. Find and correct them.

5 Read the letter and correct it.

1 Mark where each paragraph ends.
2 Correct seven mistakes (punctuation and capital letters).
3 Write a greeting and an ending.

.... Mrs Gordon.
i'm writing to say thank you for having me. I had a fantastic time in Chicago, I've told my family all about it. I think the best bit was our visit to Lake Michigan. Also, I really enjoyed the musical 'Million Dollar Quartet' at the theatre. It was brilliant. Mum and Dad would love you and your family to come and visit us in cambridge. perhaps you could come next summer. What do you think.
Once again, thank you so much and please keep in touch.

..............,
lisa

Your turn

6 Imagine you've spent three months with a host family in London. Write a thank you letter. Mention some of the things you enjoyed doing during your stay. Choose from the list below.

• go on a day trip to Brighton
• visit the Tower of London
• go to the funfair at Chessington World of Adventures
• ride on the London Eye
• take a river boat to Greenwich
• see a Shakespeare play at the Globe Theatre
• see the lions at Woburn Safari Park

> Now turn to page 95 in the Activity Book.

QUIZ TIME

Inventions that changed the world

How much do you know about these inventions?

1 **When was the printing press invented?**

   A 1800 B 1220 C 1650 D (1440)

3 **What invention from 1969 lets you talk to your friends online?**

   A home computer B smartphone C Internet
   D keyboard

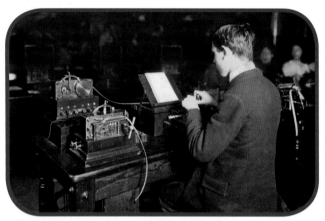

2 **Which of these fast methods of communication came first?**

   A telegraph B telephone C email D Internet

4 **Which material is used in all these products: clothes, keyboards, bottles, phones, computers, planes and cars?**

   A glass B plastic C gold D aluminium

1 The printing press was invented in 1440 by Johannes Gutenberg, who was born in Mainz, Germany. Before it was invented, there were very few books. Most books had to be copied by hand so they were very expensive. Today, over 300,000 books are published every year in the USA alone.

2 The telegraph was the first really fast method of communicating over long distances. Electricity made wireless telegraphy possible in the late 19th and early 20th centuries. Before the telegraph was invented, people had to send letters by post to get in touch.

3 In 1969 one computer communicated with another computer and the Internet was born. Early computers could not communicate with each other. The World Wide Web (WWW) is an application of the Internet. It was created in 1989 by British scientist Tim Berners-Lee.

4 Plastics are used in a huge range of products today, like planes and phones. They are light, cheap, strong and flexible. Modern methods of communication were made possible by the use of plastics. The English inventor Alexander Parkes created the earliest form of manmade plastic in 1855.

My score: ....   4 correct answers: **Well done!**   3 correct answers: **Not bad!**   0–2 correct answers: **Try again!**

New words

by hand   copy   create   flexible
manmade (plastics)   method   printing press
product   range (of products)   telegraph
(wireless) telegraphy

Reading

1 (3/23) Listen and read. Do the quiz.

2 (3/24) Listen and read the answers. What's your score?

Study tip

Scanning for specific information

You scan a text to find information such as names of people and places, dates, countries and nationalities. Look for capital letters, numbers and names of countries or nationalities.

3 Scan the answers to the quiz questions on page 94. How quickly can you find and circle this information?

1 Who was the printing press invented by?
2 How many books are published in the USA every year?
3 When did wireless telegraphy become possible?
4 In what year was the WWW created?
5 What nationality is Tim Berners-Lee?
6 Who created the first manmade form of plastic?

Comprehension

4 Read again and match the inventions with their benefits.

1 This invention allows people to communicate online whenever they want ....
2 Thanks to this invention, cars and planes are lighter, so we can travel further but use less petrol. ....
3 Before this was invented, people had to write letters to keep in touch. ....
4 Thanks to this invention, books became much cheaper to make. ....

Listening

5 (3/25) Listen to a Science teacher talking about electricity with her class. Match 1–5 with a–g. There are two extra options.

Benjamin Franklin experiments with a kite.

1 Electricity is found   a invented electricity.
2 Benjamin Franklin   b only exist because of
3 Many inventors   electricity.
  and scientists   c in nature.
4 Thomas Edison   d proved that lightning is
5 Many important   electrical.
  inventions   e invented TV and computers.
                             f invented the first modern
                                light bulb.
                             g tried to use electricity to
                                make light.

Speaking

6 In pairs, match the inventions (1–6) with their benefits (a–f). Which do you think is the most/least important invention?

1 light bulbs [c]   4 fridges [ ]
2 wind power [ ]   5 social networking [ ]
3 mass-produced cars [ ]   6 GPS technology [ ]

a We can buy food and keep it fresh for longer.
b We can keep in touch with friends anywhere.
c We don't have to go to bed when it gets dark.
d It's clean, cheap and it reduces pollution.
e We can find our destination easily.
f We can travel further and go at our own speed.

Think about it

Make your own list of the top five inventions that have changed the world. What benefits have they brought?

Writing: An important invention

7 Choose an invention that you think is important. Find a photo or a picture and write about it.

E Revision

1 Match two words from the box with each picture.

aluminium	bag	~~bin~~	bottle	box	can
cardboard	crisp	fleece	glass	jumper	
packet	plastic	pot	~~rubbish~~	yoghurt	

1 *rubbish bin*

2 Complete the text with the present simple passive form of the verbs.

Every year, tons of old clothes ¹ *are thrown* (throw) away with other waste from our homes. Up to 95 percent of these clothes could be reused or recycled. The fashion company H&M has begun a global recycling programme. Shoppers ² .... (allow) to hand in their old clothes at any H&M store. Any pieces of clothing of any brand ³ .... (accept).

If they bring a carrier bag full of clothes, customers ⁴ .... (give) a voucher for £5.

H&M say, 'We want to do good for the environment.' The company was started in Sweden in 1947. It now has over 2,700 shops in forty-eight countries.

80 percent of old clothes that are collected are reused. They ⁵ .... (send) to many countries in Europe, Africa and Asia. They ⁶ .... (check) and sorted and the best ⁷ .... (sell) in secondhand shops and markets.

The other 20 percent of old clothes are recycled. Recycled textiles ⁸ .... (use) to make new things such as blankets, mattresses and gardening products.

3 Complete the text with the verbs in the box. Use the present simple passive.

collect	donate	give	make	make	separate
~~not throw~~	use	wash			

Some things you didn't know you can recycle!

Here are some surprising things that can be reused or recycled.

In Japan, false teeth ¹ *aren't thrown* away! A company recycles the metal inside them. The company sells the metal and the money ² .... to the charity UNICEF (United Nations International Children's Emergency Fund).

Old trainers are never too old. First, they ³ ...., then they ⁴ .... to people who don't have enough money to buy new trainers or they ⁵ .... into building materials.

In some hair salons, the hair that your hairdresser cuts off ⁶ .... by a company called Locks of Love. It ⁷ .... to make wigs for people who are ill.

Old mobile phones, laptops and other electronic devices are full of valuable materials like gold, steel and plastic. These materials ⁸ .... at a Reprocessing Centre and then each material ⁹ .... into something new.

4 Write and ask questions about the inventions. Use the information in the table to answer them.

1 **A:** *When was the telephone invented?*
   B: *It was invented in 1875 by Alexander Graham Bell.*

1 When / telephone / invent?
2 When / first / incandescent light bulb / develop?
3 Who / first / mass-produced cars / build by?
4 Who / World Wide Web / create by?
5 Who / iPhone / invent by?

What?	Who?	When?
1 telephone	Alexander Graham Bell	1875
2 first incandescent light bulb	Thomas Edison	1879
3 mass-produced cars	Henry Ford	1908
4 World Wide Web	Tim Berners-Lee	1989
5 iPhone	Steve Jobs	2007

5 Read the dialogue and choose the correct words.

Dylan: Are you ¹(excited)/ exciting about going home?

Tom: I can't wait to see Mum and Dad but I'm going to be ² boring / bored on the flight home. It's about eight hours. The films on the way here were very ³ bored / boring. They were all ones I've seen before.

Dylan: I'm not ⁴ surprised / surprising. You've seen everything! So what will you tell your family about England?

Tom: The weather isn't brilliant but I've had a really ⁵ interested / interesting time. I've really enjoyed myself.

Dylan: What were the best things you did?

Tom: We've done lots of ⁶ excited / exciting things. I loved getting close to the lions at Woburn Safari Park.

Dylan: But you were really ⁷ frightened / frightening!

Tom: No, I wasn't!

6 Tom is saying goodbye to his rugby coach. Complete the dialogue. Then act it out.

Tom: Well, bye Mr Patterson. ¹ _Thank you for everything_. You've been a great coach.

Mr Patterson: It was a pleasure. The rugby team is going to ² .... We won a lot of matches this year!

Tom: Well, it's a shame I can't say goodbye to everyone. Please give ³ .... to them all.

Mr Patterson: Yes, I will and please ⁴ .... again.

Tom: Well, I'd like to come back next summer.

Mr Patterson: Oh, the rugby season will be over. Never mind, keep ⁵ .... with the other team members. And have a ⁶ ....

Tom: Thanks, I will.

7 Read the letter and correct it.

1 Number the paragraphs in the correct order.
2 Find and correct nine mistakes (punctuation and capital letters).
3 Write a greeting and an ending.

> .... Aunt Cora,
>
> **A** ☐ my host family, the joneses, lived in Cambridge? I was really well looked after. I was taken to London and I was taken camping. I even learnt how to play rugby. It was great and I made friends with really nice people,
>
> **B** ☐ So. thank you again because Mum only allowed me to go because of you. Give my regards to Uncle thomas.
>
> **C** ☐ I'm writing to say thank you for telling me about the school exchange programme. I've just come back from three months in england and it was fantastic
>
> ....,
>
> Tom

Pronunciation: /r/

8 Listen and repeat.
Ron gets on a **r**ubbish t**r**uck
Then his **r**outine begins.
He so**r**ts out your **r**ecycling
And **r**eturns the empty bins.

9 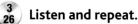 Listen and repeat the tongue twisters again and again very fast.

1 Red roses are really romantic.
2 Red lorry, yellow lorry.
3 Rocky ran round the room three times.
4 Richard rode the wrong ride at the funfair.
5 Reduce, reuse, recycle.

10 Read and tick (✓).

I can:	
identify materials and containers. *Boxes are usually made of cardboard.*	☐
describe processes. *The bottles are collected in bottle banks.*	☐
express opinions and describe feelings. *The film is boring. She's bored.*	☐
report past events. *A forty-two-year-old was saved by a six-year-old.*	☐
say goodbye. *Please come and see us again soon.*	☐

> Turn to Unit 8 Check in the Activity Book on page 96.

pick and mix

Game on!

Play the *Today!* big board game.

Instructions

You'll need:
- a counter for each player
- a pair of dice
- a watch for each group

How to play
- Play this game in groups of three or four.
- First, make your counter. Take a piece of paper and cut out a small circle. Write your name on it.
- Read the instructions below to find out what you have to do.
- Start the game. Roll the dice and go forward as many squares as the dice indicate. Do what the square says.
- The winner is the person who finishes first!

What you have to do

Orange squares: Talk for thirty seconds. Then go forward three squares. If you can't talk for the full thirty seconds, go back one square.

Green squares: Answer the question. If you answer correctly using your book, stay where you are. If you answer correctly without looking at the book, go forward two squares. If you answer incorrectly, go back two squares.

Purple squares: Complete the sentence within five seconds. Then go forward one square. If you take longer, stay where you are.

Yellow squares: Name five items in fifteen seconds! If you can't, go back three squares.

Blue squares: Complete the joke! Then go forward one square. If you can't complete the joke, stay where you are.

START

1 Talk about your family.

10 Talk about your plans for next weekend.

9 Name five injuries or illnesses.

11 What has Ella Vine wanted to do for a long time? [U5B]

12 I was ... when the bell rang for class today.

13 Name five parts of a building.

22 Name five containers.

21 I'm allowed to ... but I'm not allowed to ... .

23 Talk about what you like doing in your free time.

24 Who paints the fastest? Who paints the slowest? [U7A]

25 I've got lots of ... but not many ... .

2

Who's Jamie Oliver and what did he use to do when he was eight years old? [U3A]

3

TEACHER: Tell me a sentence that starts with an 'I'.
STUDENT: I is the ...
TEACHER: Stop! We .... say 'is' after 'I'. The right form is 'am'.
STUDENT: OK. I am the ninth letter of the alphabet!

4

When I was three years old I couldn't ... .

5

Name five outdoor activities.

8

My dad has never ... .

7

Who's Steve Backshall and how many countries has he visited? [U4B]

6

Talk about what life will be like in the year 2050.

14

MUM: Did you enjoy your first day at school?
DAUGHTER: *First* day? Do you mean I .... to go back tomorrow?

15

Talk about your favourite actor.

16

What time does Tara have to be back home on weekdays? What about at the weekend? [U6A]

17

I like clothes which ... .

20

What should you do if someone faints? [U6B]

19

Talk about your best holiday.

18

Name five wild animals.

26

What are some fleece jumpers made from? [U8A]

27

MUM: Would you .... your dinner now, dear?
SON: What are my choices?
MUM: Yes or No.

28

What food items were used to test smellovision? [U8B]

FINISH

Extra speaking practice

Unit 1B, Exercise 9

Student A

1 B is going away next weekend. Ask about his/her trip. Then write down the answers.

1 **A:** *Where are you going?*
  B: *I'm going to Manchester.*

1 where / you / go?	*Manchester*
2 when / you / leave?	....
3 how / you / travel?	....
4 what time / the train / leave?	....
5 what time / it / arrive / in Manchester?	....

2 You're going on holiday next weekend. Look at your flight details. Answer B's questions about your trip.

1 **B:** *Where are you going?*
  A: *I'm going to New York.*

E-TICKET NO:	345463728291	**E-TICKET**
FLIGHT:	EA554	
FROM:	London (Heathrow)	
TO:	New York (JFK)	
DATE:	10th Oct Dep: 14.15 Arr: 17.10	

Unit 2B, Exercise 8

Student A

1 Make predictions about the future. Use *If* + present simple. B completes the predictions.

A: *If we don't go to school to learn, ...*
B: *a: we'll study online at home.*

1 If / we / not go / to school / to learn, ...
2 If / robots / become / more intelligent than people, ...
3 If / people / live / on Mars, ...
4 If / people / live / in very high buildings, ...
5 If / a company / invent / waterproof phones, ...

2 Listen to B and complete the predictions about the future. Choose from a–e and use the future form.

B: *If your clothes can charge your phone, ...*
A: *c: you'll always be able to use it.*

a people / live / underground.
b they / not go / to other places / by plane.
c you / always / be able to use / it.
d they / be able to see / better.
e our houses / be / very clean.

Unit 3C, Exercise 8

Student A

1 Ask B about the Rosetta Stone. Then complete the information sheet.

A: *What is it?*
B: *It's ...*

The Rosetta Stone

What: ....
Where from: ....
How old: ....
Why special: ....
Where now: ....

2 Answer B's questions about the Ombra della Sera.

B: *What is it?*
A: *It's a tall, thin statue ...*

Ombra della Sera

(The Evening Shadow)

What: a tall, thin statue made of bronze

Where from: Volterra, a town in Tuscany, Italy

How old: more than 2,000 years old

Why special: very old but it looks modern

Where now: Etruscan Museum in Volterra

Unit 4A, Exercise 9

Student A

1 Ask B questions. Then complete the questionnaire.

1 A: *Have you ever been swimming in a lake?*
   B: *...*

Have you ever ...

	Yes/No	When
1 go swimming / in a lake?	☐	....
2 ride / a horse?	☐	....
3 sleep / in a tent?	☐	....
4 go / to London?	☐	....
5 join / a drama club?	☐	....

2 Complete the questionnaire for you. Then answer B's questions.

1 B: *Have you ever been sailing?*
   A: *Yes, I have. I went sailing (last summer holiday)./*
      No, I've never been sailing./No, I've never done that.

Have you ever ...

	Yes/No	When
1 go / sailing?	☐	....
2 do / a cookery course?	☐	....
3 catch / a fish?	☐	....
4 be / in a helicopter?	☐	....
5 join / a choir?	☐	....

Student A Activities

Unit 5A, Exercise 10

Student A

1 **Answer B's questions about your family's plans for a trip to Disneyland Paris.**

B: *Have you looked at the Disneyland Paris website yet?*

A: *Yes, I've already done that.*

B: *Have you ... ?*

A: *No, I haven't done that yet. I'm going to do it (tomorrow).*

> Things to do
>
> • look at the Disneyland Paris website ✓
> • decide what to see and do ✓
> • Mum and Dad — book train tickets ✓
> • buy a French phrase book ✓
> • phone French penfriend to let him/her know ✓
> • arrange to meet him/her ✓
> • decide where and when to meet ✓
> • buy new trainers ✓

2 **Ask B questions about his/her family's plans for a tour of the Harry Potter Studio and tick (✓) or cross (✗) the boxes.**

A: *Have you looked at the Harry Potter Studio Tour website yet?*

B: *Yes, I've already done that.*

A: *Have you ... ?*

B: *No, I haven't done that yet. I'm going to do it (tomorrow).*

> Things to do
>
> • look at the Harry Potter Studio Tour website ✓
> • book the date and time ☐
> • buy tickets ☐
> • check train times ☐
> • ask a friend to come, too ☐
> • read the Harry Potter books again ☐
> • watch the Harry Potter films again ☐
> • buy a Harry Potter T-shirt ☐
> • buy new trainers ☐

Unit 6B, Exercise 8

Student A

1 **Ask B for advice about your planned rafting trip and complete the information sheet.**

A: *What kind of shoes should I wear?*

B: *You shouldn't wear ordinary shoes. You should wear trainers or river sandals.*

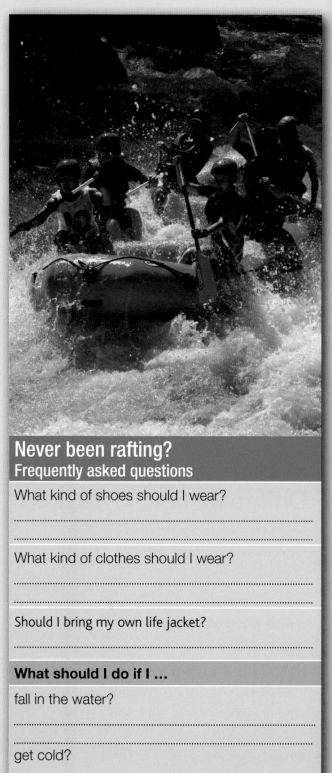

Never been rafting?
Frequently asked questions

What kind of shoes should I wear?

....

....

What kind of clothes should I wear?

....

....

Should I bring my own life jacket?

....

What should I do if I ...

fall in the water?

....

....

get cold?

....

2 Give B advice about his/her planned rock climbing course. Use the information below.

B: *Should I take food with me?*

A: *No, you shouldn't take food into the climbing area.*

Never been rock climbing?
Frequently asked questions

Should I ...	You should .../ You shouldn't ...
take food with me?	take food into the climbing area. ✗
take water with me?	take bottled water. ✓
wear special clothes?	wear a skirt or tight jeans. ✗
	wear comfortable clothes. ✓
What kind of shoes should I wear?	wear climbing boots or trainers. ✓
What should I do if I fall and sprain my ankle?	take your boots or trainers off. ✗
	call the climbing instructor. ✓

Unit 7A, Exercise 8

Student A

1 You're B's grandmother/grandfather. Make comments.

1 A: *I can't hear what you're saying.*
  B: *OK, I'll speak more loudly.*

1 I can't hear what you're saying.
2 Why are you sitting so far away?
3 I'm pushing the door but it won't open!
4 You're making a mess! There's paint everywhere!
5 You went to bed late yesterday!
6 You're walking too fast!

2 You're B's friend. Respond to B's comments. Choose from a–f.

1 B: *We played badly today and we lost the match!*
  A: *Don't worry, you'll do better next time.*

a Sorry, we / can't play / the music / loudly than that
b You / have to look at / them / carefully
c I / can't eat / quickly!
d I / do / badly than you!
e OK, we / run / far tomorrow
f Don't worry, you / do / well next time

Unit 8A, Exercise 8

Student A

1 Explain to B how glass is recycled. Use the diagram, the prompts and the present simple passive.

1 *Bottles and jars are collected in bottle banks.*

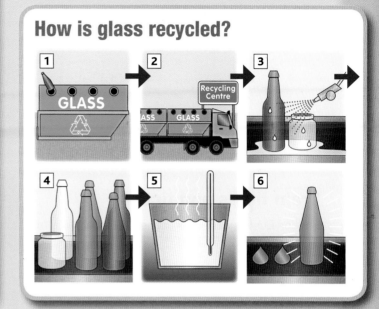

How is glass recycled?

1 bottles and jars / collect / in bottle banks
2 they / take / to Recycling Centre
3 first / the bottles and jars / wash
4 next / they / sort into / colours
5 then / the clean bottles and jars / melt / at 750 degrees Centigrade
6 finally / the melted glass / make into / new bottles

2 Listen to B explaining how aluminium cans are recycled. Put the pictures in the correct order.

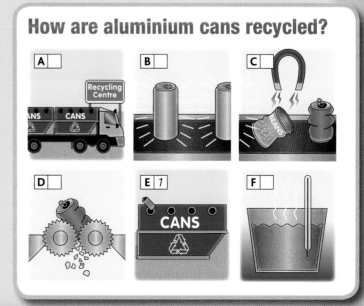

How are aluminium cans recycled?

Extra speaking practice

Unit 1B, Exercise 9

Student B

1 You're going away next weekend. Look at your train ticket and timetable. Answer A's questions about your trip.

1 A: *Where are you going?*
B: *I'm going to Manchester.*

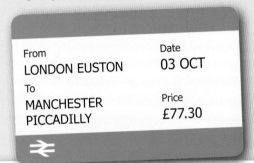

From LONDON EUSTON	Date 03 OCT
To MANCHESTER PICCADILLY	Price £77.30

Train times and tickets

London Euston [EUS] to Manchester Piccadilly [MAN]

Outward 3 Oct

Dep.	From	To	Arr.	Dur.
15.20	London Euston [EUS] Platform 14	Manchester Piccadilly [MAN] Platform 7	17.28	2hr 08m

2 A is going on holiday next weekend. Ask about his/her holiday. Then write down the answers.

1 B: *Where are you going?*
A: *I'm going to New York.*

1 where / you / go?   ...New York...
2 when / you / leave?   ....
3 how / you / travel?   ....
4 what time / your plane / take off?   ....
5 what time / it / land / in New York?   ....

Unit 2B, Exercise 8

Student B

1 Listen to A and complete the predictions about the future. Choose from a–e and use the future form.

A: *If we don't go to school to learn, ...*
B: *a: we'll study online at home.*

a we / study online / at home.
b they / go / to Earth / on holiday.
c they / be able to see / for kilometres.
d we / be able to text / underwater.
e they / be / more important than people.

2 Make predictions about the future. Use *If* + present simple. A completes the predictions.

B: *If your clothes can charge your phone, ...*
A: *c: you'll always be able to use it.*

1 If / your clothes / can charge / your phone, ...
2 If / people / have / bionic eyes, ...
3 If / the world / get / too hot, ...
4 If / a robot / do / the household jobs, ...
5 If / people / have / virtual holidays, ...

Unit 3C, Exercise 8

Student B

1 Answer A's questions about the Rosetta Stone.

A: *What is it?*

B: *It's a large, black stone ...*

The Rosetta Stone

What: a large, black stone; the front is smooth, the back is rough. It has writing in ancient Egyptian and Greek alphabets on it.

Where from: Egypt, near a town called Rosetta

How old: more than 2,000 years old

Why special: helped people understand ancient Egyptian

Where now: British Museum, London

2 Ask A about the Ombra della Sera. Then complete the information sheet.

B: *What is it?*

A: *It's ...*

Ombra della Sera

(The Evening Shadow)

What: ....

Where from: ....

How old: ....

Why special: ....

Where now: ....

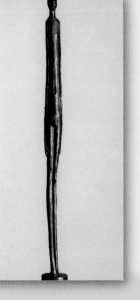

Unit 4A, Exercise 9

Student B

1 Complete the questionnaire for you. Then answer A's questions.

1 A: *Have you ever been swimming in a lake?*

   B: *Yes, I have. I went swimming in a lake (a month ago)./No, I've never been swimming in a lake./No, I've never done that.*

Have you ever ...

	Yes/No	When
1 go swimming / in a lake?	☐	....
2 ride / a horse?	☐	....
3 sleep / in a tent?	☐	....
4 go / to London?	☐	....
5 join / a drama club?	☐	....

2 Ask A questions. Then complete the questionnaire.

1 B: *Have you ever been sailing?*

   A: *...*

Have you ever ...

	Yes/No	When
1 go / sailing?	☐	....
2 do / a cookery course?	☐	....
3 catch / a fish?	☐	....
4 be / in a helicopter?	☐	....
5 join / a choir?	☐	....

Student B Activities

Unit 5A, Exercise 10

Student B

1 Ask A questions about his/her family's plans for a trip to Disneyland Paris and tick (✓) or cross (✗) the boxes.

B: *Have you looked at the Disneyland Paris website yet?*

A: *Yes, I've already done that.*

B: *Have you ... ?*

A: *No, I haven't done that yet. I'm going to do it (tomorrow).*

Things to do

- look at the Disneyland Paris website ✓
- decide what to see and do ☐
- Mum and Dad – book train tickets ☐
- buy a French phrase book ☐
- phone French penfriend to let him/her know ☐
- arrange to meet him/her ☐
- decide where and when to meet ☐
- buy new trainers ☐

---

2 Answer A's questions about your family's plans for a tour of the Harry Potter Studio during a trip to London.

A: *Have you looked at the Harry Potter Studio Tour website yet?*

B: *Yes, I've already done that.*

A: *Have you ... ?*

B: *No, I haven't done that yet. I'm going to do it (tomorrow).*

Things to do

- look at the Harry Potter Studio Tour website ✓
- book the date and time ✓
- buy tickets ✓
- check train times ✗
- ask a friend to come too ✗
- read the Harry Potter books again ✓
- watch the Harry Potter films again ✗
- buy a Harry Potter T-shirt ✗
- buy new trainers ✗

BOOK YOUR DATE AND TIME NOW

Tickets must be purchased in advance.
No tickets are sold at the Studio Tour.

Unit 6B, Exercise 8

Student B

1 Give A advice about his/her planned rafting trip. Use the information below.

A: *What kind of shoes should I wear?*

B: *You shouldn't wear ordinary shoes. You should wear trainers or river sandals.*

Never been rafting?
Frequently asked questions

	You should …/You shouldn't …
What kind of shoes should I wear?	wear ordinary shoes. ✗ wear trainers or river sandals. ✓
What kind of clothes should I wear?	wear cotton T-shirts or jeans. ✗ wear a wetsuit and a wool hat to keep warm. ✓
Should I bring my own life jacket?	bring your own. ✗ The company provides life jackets and helmets.
What should I do if I …	
fall in the water?	panic. ✗ try to keep your head above water and wait for help. ✓
get cold?	bring a woollen jumper or fleece so you don't get cold. ✓

2 Ask A for advice about your planned rock climbing course and complete the information sheet.

B: *Should I take food with me?*

A: *No, you shouldn't take food into the climbing area.*

Never been rock climbing?
Frequently asked questions

Should I …

take food with me?

....

take water with me?

....

wear special clothes?

....

....

What kind of shoes should I wear?

....

What should I do if I fall and sprain my ankle?

....

....

Unit 7A, Exercise 8

Student B

1 You're A's grandson/granddaughter. Respond to A's comments. Choose from a–f.

1 A: *I can't hear what you're saying.*
B: *OK, I'll speak more loudly.*

a Sorry, I / paint / carefully

b You / have to push / hard

c Sorry, I / sit / near to you

d Sorry, I / walk / slowly

e OK, I / speak / loudly

f Don't worry, I / go to bed / early today

2 You're A's friend. Make comments.

1 B: *We played badly today and we lost the match!*
A: *Don't worry, you'll do better next time.*

1 We played badly today and we lost the match!

2 The music at this party is very quiet. I can't hear it!

3 We need more exercise. We didn't run very far today.

4 I didn't do well in the Maths test!

5 Finish your breakfast. We're going to be late!

6 I can't see the difference between these pictures.

Unit 8A, Exercise 8

Student B

1 Listen to A explaining how glass is recycled. Put the pictures in the correct order.

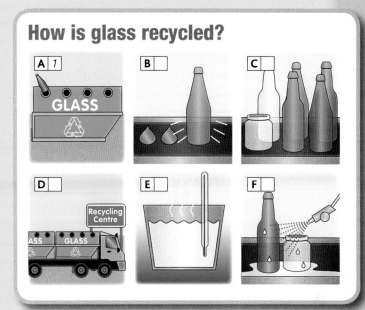

2 Explain to A how aluminium cans are recycled. Use the diagram, the prompts and the present simple passive.

1 *The cans are collected in recycling banks.*

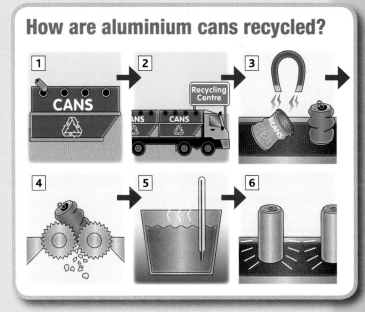

1 cans / collect / in recycling banks

2 they / take / to Recycling Centre

3 first / the aluminium cans / separate / from other metals / with magnets

4 then / the aluminium / cut into / small pieces

5 next / the pieces / melt / at 750 degrees Centigrade.

6 finally / the melted aluminium / make into / new cans

Word list

Unit 1

Lesson A

Appearance:
attractive
curly
dark
fair
good-looking
long
old
short
slim
straight
tall
young

Personality adjectives:
bossy
cheerful
clever
creative
generous
grumpy
hard-working
honest
lazy
patient
polite
rude
selfish
shy
sociable

Lesson B

Transport:
boat
bus
car
coach
helicopter
plane
underground train

Travel expressions:
arrive
catch (the bus/plane)
check in (your luggage)
collect (your luggage)
get off (the bus/train)
get on (the bus/train)
go through security
land
leave
miss (the bus/plane)
show (your passport)
take off

Lesson C

Free time activities:
do a (cookery) course
do drama
do judo
do karate
do mountain biking
do orienteering
do photography
do water sports
go camping
go dancing
go kayaking
go sightseeing
go to the cinema
go to the park
join a (chess/drama/reading) club
join the choir
play chess
play computer games
play an instrument (the guitar)
play sports (basketball, rugby, volleyball)
sign up for a (climbing) course
sing (in a choir)

Unit 2

Lesson A

Technology:
app
(mobile phone) charger
digital camera
electric bike
games console
laptop
(TV) remote control
robot
(bendy) smartphone
solar panels
tablet computer
virtual (games)
wi-fi

Lesson B

Using technology:

Nouns
battery
contacts (list)
e-book reader
email address
icon
keyboard
mouse
online game
plug
printer
screen
transformer
USB cable
website

Verbs
click (on)
delete
download
log on
plug in/unplug
print
save
send (emails, photographs)
shut down
surf the Internet
switch off/on

Unit 3

Lesson A

Education and work:
become famous/successful
do well at school
earn a living/money
find/get a job (as a chef)
get a degree/diploma
go to college/university
leave school
pass exams
start school
study hard
work hard

Lesson B

Prepositions of movement:
across
along
around
into
out of
over
through
towards
under

Lesson C

Describing objects:
bronze
gold
hard
large
long
rectangular
rough
round
silver
smooth
soft
square
straight
thick
thin

Unit 4

Lesson A

Camping and survival skills:
build a raft/shelter
catch a fish
cook (food) over an open fire
go camping/hiking/horse-riding/rafting/
   rock climbing/sailing
light a fire
put up a tent
read a map
ride a horse
sail a boat
see (a bear)
sleep in a tent/under the stars
track wild animals

Lesson B

Adjectives describing qualities:

active
adventurous
brave
careful
energetic
fearless
fit
healthy
inspiring
passionate (about)
strong

Unit 5

Lesson A

Film types:

action/adventure film
animated film/cartoon
comedy
drama
fantasy film
historical film
horror film
musical
science fiction
thriller

Lesson B

Films:

People
actor
cameraman
cast
character
director
make-up artist
(film) star

What happens
ending
plot/story
scene
special effects

Lesson C

Free time activities:

babysit (for my parents/relatives)
chat online
do jobs around the house
hang out with friends
have a sleepover
IM (instant message)
make playlists
play (board/online) games
read books/e-books
shop (online)
stay in
stay up (late)
text (my) friends

volunteer (at an animal shelter)/do
    volunteer work
watch DVDs

Unit 6

Lesson A

Household jobs:

clear (the table)
do (the washing-up)
feed (the dog)
lay (the table)
load (the dishwasher)
make (my bed)
tidy (my room)
vacuum (my room)
walk (the dog)
water (the plants)

Lesson B

Injuries, illnesses and treatments:

Injuries and illnesses
break your arm/leg
catch/have a stomach bug
cut yourself
faint
have sunburn
pull a muscle
sprain your ankle/wrist

Treatments
call an ambulance
clean it
drink lots of water
keep (it) cool/warm
put a bandage on it
put cream on it
put an ice pack on it
put a plaster on it
rest

Unit 7

Lesson A

Adverbs:

badly
carefully
carelessly
early
far
fast
hard
late
loudly
near
quickly
quietly
slowly
well

Lesson B

Buildings and parts of buildings:

block of flats
ceiling
door
flat
(ground, first, second, top) floor
house
office
palace
roof
room
skyscraper
stairs
theatre
wall
window

Lesson C

Wild animals:

camel
cheetah
giraffe
lemur
lion
monkey
penguin
rhinoceros (rhino)
tiger
zebra

Unit 8

Lesson A

Containers and materials:

aluminium (can)
(carrier) bag
bin
bottle
box
can (of cola)
cardboard
(juice/milk) carton
glass
jar
packet (of biscuits/crisps)
paper
plastic
(yoghurt) pot
steel
tin (of baked beans)

Lesson B

Adjectives with -ed/-ing endings:

amused/amusing
annoyed/annoying
bored/boring
embarrassed/embarrassing
excited/exciting
frightened/frightening
interested/interesting
surprised/surprising

Andy's grammar lessons

1 Present simple

Positive

I go to school every day.
You **play** football at weekends.
He **watches** TV in his free time.
We **live** in Chicago.
You **live** in Cambridge.
They **drive** a big car.

Negative

I **don't like** rugby.
You **don't play** basketball.
She **doesn't speak** English
We **don't go** to school.
You **don't work** in a hospital.
They **don't have** a dog.

Questions and short answers

Do I **look** OK?	Yes, you **do**./No, you **don't**.
Do you **live** in a house?	Yes, I **do**./No, I **don't**.
Does she **work** with children?	Yes, she **does**./No, she **doesn't**.
Do we **sing** every day?	Yes, you **do**./No, you **don't**.
Do you **play** rugby?	Yes, we **do**./No, we **don't**.
Do they **go** to college?	Yes, they **do**./No, they **don't**.

Wh- questions

Where do you **live**?	I **live** in York.
When does she **work**?	She **works** on Mondays.
How do they **get** to school?	They **go** by bike.

2 Adverbs of frequency

always ****   usually ***   often **   sometimes *   never

Positive

I'm **always** sociable.
Jack is **usually** polite.
She **often makes** cakes.
He **sometimes works** at weekends.
They are **never** rude.

Negative

I **don't always play** computer games in the evenings.
He **doesn't usually play** basketball on Sundays.
They **don't often go** on holiday.

3 Present continuous

Positive

I'm **singing** loudly.
You're **doing** your homework.
The dog is **jumping** up and down.
She's **walking** to school.
We're **playing** rugby at the moment.
You're **living** at home.
They're **having** dinner.

Negative

I'm **not working** at the moment.
You **aren't watching** that programme.
She **isn't sitting** on my chair.
We **aren't living** in New York.
You **aren't smiling**.
They **aren't doing** anything.

Questions and short answers

Am I **making** a pirate ship cake?	Yes, you **are**./No, you **aren't**.
Are you **playing** a game?	Yes, I **am**./No, I'm **not**.
Is he **feeling** grumpy now?	Yes, he **is**./No, he **isn't**.
Are we **being** rude?	Yes, you **are**./No, you **aren't**.
Are you **drinking** water?	Yes, I **am**./No, I'm **not**.
Are they **smiling**?	Yes, they **are**./No, they **aren't**.

Wh- questions

What am I **watching**?	You're **watching** a TV programme.
Where's he **going**?	He's **going** home.
Where are we **sleeping**?	You're **sleeping** here.

4 Present continuous for future arrangements

Positive

I'm **meeting** my friend tomorrow.
We're **travelling** to Spain next summer.
They're **going** camping in a month.

Negative

You **aren't arriving** next Tuesday.
She **isn't watching** the match on Saturday.
They **aren't travelling** to the airport by coach.

Questions and short answers

Am I **leaving** in the morning?
Yes, you **are**./No, you **aren't**.

Is it **taking off** soon?
Yes, it **is**./No, it **isn't**.

Are you **meeting** him at the airport?
Yes, we **are**./No, we **aren't**.

Wh- questions

When's Peter **playing** basketball?
He's **playing** on Sunday.

Where are they **meeting** tonight?
They're **meeting** at the cinema?

Who's she **visiting** in Italy next week?
She's **visiting** her friend Susan.

5 Present simple for fixed timetables

The plane **takes off** at 10.00 a.m.
The helicopter **lands** at 11.30 p.m.
The train **doesn't arrive** until 2.30 p.m.

Wh- questions

What time **does** the bus **arrive?**
It **arrives** at 10.30 a.m.

When does the flight check-in **open?**
It **opens** two hours before the flight.

When does the plane **take off?**
It **doesn't take off** until 7.15 p.m.

6 *going to* for future plans

Positive

I'm **going to** visit New York.
You're **going to** drive home.
He's **going to** cook dinner.
We're **going to** join the choir.
You're **going to** play the guitar.
They're **going to** do a cookery course.

Negative

I'm **not going to** go sightseeing.
You **aren't going to** play chess.
She **isn't going to** join the choir this year.
We **aren't going to** go kayaking.
You **aren't going to** play volleyball.
They **aren't going to** go dancing.

Questions and short answers

Am I **going to** travel by coach?
Yes, you **are.**/No, you **aren't.**

Are we **going to** drive through London?
Yes, you **are.**/No, you **aren't.**

Are you **going to** come for dinner?
Yes, we **are.**/No, we **aren't.**

Wh- questions

What are you **going to** do?
I'm **going to** play the piano.

Who's he **going to** meet?
He's **going to** meet his mum.

Where are they **going to** stay?
They're **going to** stay with their aunt.

7 Future predictions with *will/won't*

Positive

I'll **have** a robot!
You'll **have** a virtual holiday.
The television **will be** connected to the Internet.
We'll **be able to** fly to school.
You'll **do** all your shopping online.
They'll **drive** electric cars.

Negative

won't = will not
I **won't go** on holiday.
You **won't have** a robot.
He **won't buy** bionic eyes.
We **won't go** to school.
You **won't have** a teacher.
They **won't learn** in schools.

Questions and short answers

Will you **ride** a bike?
Yes, I **will.**/No, I **won't.**

Will she **have** a super-thin phone?
Yes, she **will.**/No, she **won't.**

Will we **live** in high buildings?
Yes, you **will.**/No, you **won't.**

Wh- questions

When will I **get** a digital camera?
You'll **get** a digital camera soon.

Where will you **live** in ten years' time?
We'll **live** in Madrid.

What will people **wear** in twenty years' time?
They'll **wear** solar-powered clothes.

8 First conditional with *will/won't*

If + present simple + *will/won't*

If I **switch off** the printer, I'll **save** electricity.
If you **surf** the Internet, you'll **find** the answer.
If she **doesn't send** the email, he **won't see** her photos.
If we've **got** her email address, we'll **contact** her.
If you **download** the game, you'll **have** fun.
If they **don't plug in** the printer, they **won't be able** to print the tickets.

Questions and short answers

If I **press** this button, **will** the computer **shut down?**
Yes, it **will.**/No, it **won't.**

If he **goes** on this website, **will** he **find** the information?
Yes, he **will.**/No, he **won't.**

If the computer **crashes, will** I **lose** my work?
Yes, you **will.**/No, you **won't.**

Wh- questions

What will happen if I **click** on this?
The teacher **will give** you more homework.

What will they **do** if they **don't have** to go to school?
They'll **study** at home.

When will I **arrive** in London if I **leave** now?
You'll **arrive** at 9.30 p.m.

9 Past simple

Positive

I **did** well at school.
You **decided** to do your homework at 5.00.
She **started** cooking last year.
We **went** to college together.
You **loved** that toy.
They **left** school at sixteen.

Negative

I **didn't like** unusual food.
You **didn't study** hard.
That new TV series **didn't start** last night.
We **didn't do** well at school.
You **didn't become** a chef.
They **didn't have** a restaurant.

Questions and short answers

Did I **enjoy** the meal?
Yes, you **did**./No, you **didn't**.

Did it **finish** early?
Yes, it **did**./No, it **didn't**.

Did you **go** to that school?
Yes, we **did**./No, we **didn't**.

Wh- questions

Where did you **go** to university?
I **went** to university in London.

What did we **have** for dinner?
You **had** chicken and potatoes.

When did they **leave** school?
They **left** school at 4 o'clock.

10 *used to*

Positive

I **used to go** to school by bike.
You **used to like** pop music.
She **used to work** hard.
We **used to go** to that school.
You **used to love** this song.
They **used to be** fussy about food.

Negative

I **didn't use to eat** fish.
You **didn't use to listen** to reggae music.
He **didn't use to help** in his parents' shop.
We **didn't use to go** camping.
You **didn't use to ride** your bike.
They **didn't use to tidy** their room.

11 *could*

Positive

I **could speak** three languages when I was five.
You **could run** ten kilometres.
It **could run** very fast.
We **could use** a computer when we were six.
You **could play** football when you were three.
They **could read** when they were four.

Negative

I **couldn't play** that game.
You **couldn't make** cakes last year.
He **couldn't get** a job.
We **couldn't speak** English.
You **couldn't make** coffee.
They **couldn't understand** the game.

Questions and short answers

Could I **play** football?
Yes, you **could**./No, you **couldn't**.

Could you **speak** French?
Yes, I **could**./No, I **couldn't**.

Could he **cook** when he was fifteen?
Yes, he **could**./No, he **couldn't**.

Could we **use** a computer?
Yes, you **could**./No, you **couldn't**.

Could you **make** cakes?
Yes, we **could**./No, we **couldn't**.

Could they **take** good photos?
Yes, they **could**./No, they **couldn't**.

12 Past continuous

Positive

I **was looking** at the pictures.
You **were walking** along the road.
She **was crossing** the road.
We **were watching** TV.
You **were pushing** your bike through the park.
They **were looking** over the wall.

Negative

I **wasn't doing** my homework.
You **weren't listening** to the teacher.
He **wasn't waiting** at the bus stop.
We **weren't looking** at the books.
You **weren't standing** in the restaurant.
They **weren't watching** a film.

Questions and short answers

Was I **walking** through the park?
Yes, you **were**./No, you **weren't**.

Were you **standing** in the garden?
Yes, I **was**./No, I **wasn't**.

Was she **running** across the road?
Yes, she **was**./No, she **wasn't**.

Were we **doing** something embarrassing?
Yes, you **were**./No, you **weren't**.

Were you **playing** your guitars?
Yes, we **were**./No, we **weren't**.

Were they **watching** the film?
Yes, they **were**./No, they **weren't**.

Wh- questions

What were you **doing** at 8.00 p.m. yesterday?
I **was getting** ready for the party.

When was he **watching** TV?
He **was watching** TV at lunchtime.

Where were they **having** lunch?
They **were having** lunch in a diner.

13 Past continuous with *when* and *while*

While they were watching the film, the lights went out.
They were watching the film **when the lights went out**.

While he was sitting in the restaurant, he heard a loud noise.
He was sitting in the restaurant **when he heard** a loud noise.

While you were doing your homework, your friend called.
You were doing your homework **when your friend** called.

14 Indefinite pronouns

Positive		Negative	Questions
somewhere	everywhere	nowhere	anywhere
something	everything	nothing	anything
someone	everyone	no one	anyone

Let's find **somewhere** to have lunch.
I want **something** to eat.
Someone is sliding down very fast.
He travels **everywhere** in his truck.
The restaurant had **everything** we wanted.
I told **everyone** about the large heart-shaped box.
That cat has got **nowhere** to sleep.
There was **nothing** in the bag.
No one helped the man.
There isn't **anywhere** to sit.
Have you got **anything** to wear for the wedding?
Is **anyone** sitting in the truck?

15 Present perfect simple with *ever* and *never*

Questions and short answers

Have I **ever** been to London?
Yes, you **have**./No, you **haven't**.

Have you **ever** tracked wild animals?
Yes, I **have**./No, I **haven't**.

Has she **ever** put up a tent?
Yes, she **has**./No, she **hasn't**.

Have we **ever** been horse-riding?
Yes, you **have**./No, you **haven't**.

Have you **ever** built a raft?
Yes, we **have**./No, we **haven't**.

Have they **ever** sailed a boat?
Yes, they **have**./No, they **haven't**.

Negative with *never*

I've **never** seen a bear.
You've **never** done a cookery course.
She's **never** climbed a mountain.
We've **never** been to the Rocky Mountains.
You've **never** read a map.
They've **never** been rock climbing.

16 Defining relative pronouns: *who*, *that*, *where*

She's **someone who** is very fit.
This is **the boat that** I sailed in.
That's **the place where** I saw a crocodile.

17 Present perfect with *just*, *already* and *yet*

Positive

I've **just been** to a disco.
He's **just done** his homework.
We've **already seen** the musical.
They've **already planned** their evening.

Negative

You **haven't done** your homework **yet**.
She **hasn't been** to the cinema **yet**.
We **haven't seen** the science fiction film **yet**.
They **haven't had** dinner **yet**.

Questions and short answers

Have I **won** the game **yet**?   Yes, you **have**./No, you **haven't**.
Have you **done** the shopping **yet**?   Yes, I **have**./No, I **haven't**.
Has she **found** the right answer **yet**?   Yes, she **has**./No, she **hasn't**.
Have they **visited** the museum **yet**?   Yes, they **have**./No, they **haven't**.

18 Present perfect with *for*/*since*

Positive

I've **lived** here **for** ten years.
You've **lived** here **since** 2005.
We've **lived** here **for** a long time.

Negative

He **hasn't seen** her **since** yesterday.
You **haven't seen** him **for** three days.
They **haven't seen** him **since** last October.

Questions

How long **have** you **been** at this school?
I've **been** at this school **for** eight months.

19 Verb + *-ing*

I **enjoy** babysitting.
You **love** staying up late.
He **likes** playing football.
She **doesn't mind** doing household jobs.
We **can't stand** getting up early.
They **hate** playing this game.

20 *prefer*

I **prefer** listening to music **to** watching TV.
They **prefer** going out for a walk **to** staying in.

Questions

Do you **prefer** eating at home **or** going out for a meal?
Which do you **prefer**, making your own playlists **or** downloading your friends' playlists?

21 *have to* – present simple

Positive

I **have to** make my bed.
You **have to** feed the cat.
She **has to** walk the dog.
We **have to** make dinner.
You **have to** clear the table.
They **have to** water the plants.

Negative

I **don't have to** make my bed.
You **don't have to** feed the cat.
He **doesn't have to** walk the dog.
We **don't have to** make dinner.
You **don't have to** clear the table.
They **don't have to** water the plants.

Questions and short answers

Do I **have to** make my bed? — Yes, you **do**./No, you **don't**.
Do you **have to** feed the cat? — Yes, I **do**./No, I **don't**.
Does it **have to** go out? — Yes, it **does**./No, it **doesn't**.
Do we **have to** make dinner? — Yes, you **do**./No, you **don't**.
Do you **have to** clear the table? — Yes, we **do**./No, we **don't**.
Do they **have to** water the plants? — Yes, they **do**./No, they **don't**.

22 *have to* – past simple

Positive

I **had to** make my bed.
She **had to** vacuum her room.
We **had to** make dinner.
They **had to** go home.

Negative

You **didn't have to** feed the cat.
It **didn't have to** go out.
We **didn't have to** walk the dog.
They **didn't have to** water the plants.

Questions and short answers

Did I **have to** make my bed? — Yes, you **did**./No, you **didn't**.
Did she **have to** vacuum her room? — Yes, she **did**./No, she **didn't**.
Did we **have to** make dinner? — Yes, you **did**./No, you **didn't**.
Did you **have to** clear the table? — Yes, we **did**./No, we **didn't**.

23 *be allowed to*

Positive

I'm **allowed to** go out.
You're **allowed to** stay up late.
She's **allowed to** go to the party.
We're **allowed to** ride our bikes.
You're **allowed to** use this room.
They're **allowed to** have long hair.

Negative

I'm **not allowed to** go out.
You **aren't allowed to** stay up late.
She **isn't allowed to** go to the party.
We **aren't allowed to** ride our bikes.
You **aren't allowed to** use this room.
They **aren't allowed to** have long hair.

Questions and short answers

Am I **allowed to** go out? — Yes, you **are**./No, you **aren't**.
Are you **allowed to** stay up late? — Yes, I **am**./No, I'm **not**.
Is she **allowed to** go to the party? — Yes, she **is**./No, she **isn't**.
Are we **allowed to** ride our bikes? — Yes, you **are**./No, you **aren't**.
Are you **allowed to** use this room? — Yes, we **are**./No, we **aren't**.
Are they **allowed to** have long hair? — Yes, they **are**./No, they **aren't**.

24 *should/shouldn't*

Positive

I **should** call the doctor.
She **should** wash her hands.
We **should** keep warm.

Negative

You **shouldn't** put the pack next to the skin.
We **shouldn't** put cream on it.
They **shouldn't** call an ambulance.

Questions and short answers

Should you stay in bed?
Yes, I **should**./No, I **shouldn't**.

Should we drink water?
Yes, you **should**./No, you **shouldn't**.

Should they stay here?
Yes, they **should**./No, they **shouldn't**.

Wh- questions

When **should** I call the doctor?
You **should** call the doctor now.

Where **should** she put her legs?
She **should** put her legs on the bed.

What **should** you do if someone breaks their arm?
We **should** call an ambulance.

25 Comparative and superlative of adverbs

Adverb	Comparative	Superlative
quickly	more quickly	the quickest
slowly	more slowly	the slowest
hard	harder	the hardest
late	later	the latest
fast	faster	the fastest
well	better	the best
badly	worse	the worst
far	further	the furthest

Comparative

Our new house is **nearer** to the school **than** the old house.
He speaks **more loudly than** you do.

Superlative

He works **the hardest** of all the students in his class.
We walked **the furthest** of everyone.

26 Comparatives with (*not*) *as ... as, less ... than* and superlatives with *the least*

Comparative

as + adjective + *as*

Roller skating is **as dangerous as** cycling.
He's **as healthy as** I am.

not as + adjective + *as*

Walking **isn't as fun as** running.
I'm **not as tall as** you are.

less + adjective + *than*

This book is **less boring than** the one
  I read last week.
They are **less excited** about going to the
  theatre **than** going to the zoo.

Superlative

the least + adjective

Question number six was the **least difficult** of all.
It was the **least expensive** holiday I've
  ever been on.

27 Quantifiers

Countable nouns: *a lot of/ lots of, a few, one or two, not many*

The park has **a lot of/lots of** visitors at
  the weekend.
There were **a few** sandwiches on a plate.
I took **one or two** photos.
There weren't **many** people at the zoo.

Uncountable nouns: *a lot of/ lots of, a little, not much*

There was **a lot of/lots of** rain that day.
Can I have **a little** sugar in my tea, please?
I haven't got **much** money today.

too/*enough*

There were **too many** people in the
  queue so I left.
There's **too much** food! I can't eat it all.
I didn't have **enough** money with me so
  I didn't buy it.
There are **enough** cages for all the
  animals.

28 Present simple passive: *be* + past participle

Positive

I'm **asked** lots of questions.
You're **sent** a new book every month.
We're **taken** to the zoo every year.

Negative

It **isn't washed** once a week.
You **aren't invited** to the party.
They **aren't made** of plastic.

Questions and short answers

Are you **driven** to school?   Yes, I **am**./No, I'm **not**.
Is she **sent** a new book every month?   Yes, she **is**./No, she **isn't**.

Wh- questions

Where's the paper **recycled**?   How are these carrier bags **made**?

29 Past simple passive: *be* + past participle

Positive

I **was interviewed** on TV.
You **were told** to sit down.
They **were sent** to London.

Negative

She **wasn't invited** to dinner.
You **weren't told** to stand up.
We **weren't asked** to come early.

Questions and short answers

Was it **made** in Italy?   Yes, it **was**./No, it **wasn't**.
Were they **sent** to London?   Yes, they **were**./No, they **weren't**.

Wh- questions

When were you **interviewed**?   I **was interviewed** yesterday.
What was she **asked**?   She **was asked** about the machine.

30 *be* + past participle + *by*

The professor **was interviewed by** a reporter.
We **were invited by** Mr Brooks.
The letter **was posted by** the school.

Wh- questions

Who was the iPod
  invented by?
Who were they
  interviewed by?

Irregular verb forms

Verb	Past simple	Past participle	Verb	Past simple	Past participle
be	was/were	been	meet	met	met
buy	bought	bought	put	put	put
catch	caught	caught	read	read	read
come	came	come	ride	rode	ridden
do	did	done	run	ran	run
drink	drank	drunk	say	said	said
drive	drove	driven	see	saw	seen
eat	ate	eaten	send	sent	sent
feed	fed	fed	sing	sang	sung
fly	flew	flown	sit	sat	sat
find	found	found	sleep	slept	slept
get	got	got	speak	spoke	spoken
give	gave	given	stand	stood	stood
go	went	been/gone	swim	swam	swum
have	had	had	take	took	taken
hear	heard	heard	tell	told	told
keep	kept	kept	understand	understood	understood
know	knew	known	wear	wore	worn
leave	left	left	win	won	won
make	made	made	write	wrote	written

Pearson Education Limited
Edinburgh Gate
Harlow
Essex CM20 2JE
England
and Associated Companies throughout the world.

www.pearsonelt.com

First published 2014
Seventh impression 2018

ISBN: 978-1-4479-0108-2

Set in Bliss Light 11/15pt
Printed in Malaysia (CTP-VVP)

Acknowledgements
The publishers and authors would like to thank the following people
for their feedback and comments during the development of the
material:
Argentina: Alicia Artusi and Cristina Djivanian
Poland: Anna Dobrowolska, Jakub Grześkowiak, Małgorzata Kuc,
Beata Wrona

Picture Credits
The publisher would like to thank the following for their kind
permission to reproduce their photographs:

(Key: b-bottom; c-centre; l-left; r-right; t-top)

Alamy Images: Adrian Sherratt 80t, Alex Segre 94tr, Catchlight
Visual Services 84b, Classic Stock 90tr, david pearson 96cl, Derek
Trask Inv. Ltd. 103tl, 107, Design Pics Inc 64br, FirstShot 83tr, Image
Source 22b, 38l, Image Source 22b, 38l, LOOK Die Bildagentur der
Fotografen GmbH 48l, mediacolor's 40cr (inset), Odilon Dimier 61,
Patrick Eden 44b, Picture Partners 56cl, redsnapper 22c, Rob 101br,
105br, Roger Bamber 100bl, Sherab 47l, The Art Archive 94bl, Tim
E White 91br, YankeePhotography 101tr, 105tr; **ArenaPAL:** Nigel
Norrington / ArenaPAL 36br; **Caters News Agency Ltd:** catersnews.
com 32tr; **Corbis:** Aristidis Vafeiadakis 33tr, Bachrach Studios
51br, Bettman 36tl, 95, Bo Bridges 50t, Classic Stock 91bl, Colin
Mcconnell / Zuma Press 28, Denis-Huot / Hemis 47c, Kazuyoshi
Nomachi 46tr; **Creatas:** 85r; **DK Images:** Andy Crawford 70bl, Neil
Lukas 13c, Robert Vente 12r, Steve Gorton 79tr; **Fotolia.com:** adimas
70r, Andrey Bandureniko 94 (fleece), barbaliss 96tr, brozova 60tl,
bst 2012 56cr, Cammy 86cr, evron.info 102, 106, frag 79br, Gufh
83l, jscalev 85c, Ka Yann 46b, Krzysztof Wktor 85l, Kurhan 63tl,
laurenthuet 79bc, netsuthep 80cl, nyul 69, rabbit75_fot 93r, rangizzz
94 (computer), robynmac 96 (trainers), ryflip 57br, Santi Rodriguez
47r, Saskia Massink 96 (teeth), Satori 80br, Scanrail 21l, Sergey Kohl
80cr, Stephan Morris 80bl, verte 94 (bottles), Visual Concepts 94
(phone); **Getty Images:** Alinari 101bl, 105bl, Koichi Kamoshida 21cr;
Imagestate Media: Michael Duerinckx 45l; **iStockphoto:** yewkeo ;
Mark Madson: 32br; **Pearson Education Ltd:** Studio 8 49 (boy), 14l
(Dylan), Jon Barlow 4tr, 5tr, 6, 8, 10tl, 10tc, 10tr, 15bl, 18t, 20tl, 20tc,
20tr, 30t, 34tl, 34tc, 34tr, 39tl, 40 (main), 44tl, 44tc, 44tr, 52, 57c,
57cl, 58tl, 58tc, 58tr, 64tr, 67tl, 67tr, 68tl, 68tc, 68tr, 72 (1), 72 (2), 72
(3), 72 (4), 72 (5), 72 (6), 73l, 73c, 76, 82tl, 82tc, 82tr, 88, 91tr, 92tl,
92tc, 92tr, 93, 97tl, Mark Bassett 60tr, Martin Beddall 14tr, Gareth
Boden 35tl, 49 (girl), Pearson 37c; **PhotoDisc:** John Wang 11tr; **Press
Association Images:** AP Images 29br, Chris Ison / PA Archive / Press
Association Images 43, Jae .C. Hong / AP 21tr, Koji Sasahara / AP
22t; **Reuters:** Bobby Yip 32cr; **Rex Features:** Barry Gomer 81bl, Ben
Osborne / Nature Picture Library 84t, Billy Farrell / BFAnyc.com
89cr, Chris Ratcliffe 51tr, Colet-Robert / SIPA 75cl, Courtesy Everett
Collection 51tl, David Fisher 51bl, London News Pictures 42tl, Nils
Jorgensen 37tr, Sipa Press 50c, Steve Meddle 42cr; **Scholastic Ltd:**
The Hunger Games, copyright Suzanne Collins, 2008, reproduced by
permission of Scholastic Ltd. All rights reserved 59cl; **Shutterstock.
com:** 47221 11tc, Andrey Bayda 54tr, Bikeworldtravel 12l, dinkat 96br,
dotshock 70c, elwynn 79bl, James A Harris 13bl, John Hoffman 62cr,
kamira 78r, Mandy Godbehear 74, Maridav 72br, Monkey Business
Images 4br, pcruciatti 78l, Pressmaster 14l (girl), 60cl, Pressmaster
14l (girl), 60cl, Radiokafka 67cr, Rob Byron 72cl, Simone Simone
13br, Tumar 71br, Vladimir Korostyshevskiy 101tl, 105tl; **SuperStock:**
Blend Images 36bl, 56tl, Blend Images 36bl, 56tl, Cusp 60bl, Image
Source 46tc, Robert Harding Picture Library 104bl, Yuri Arcurs Media
54tr (inset); **The Kobal Collection:** 20th Century Fox / Groening,
Matt 26b (circle), 53tl, Dreamworks 26c (circle), Dreamworks
Animation 53bl, Dreamworks SKG 59tr, Marvel / Paramount 26t
(circle), The Disney Channel / Hayes, Fred 53c, Twentieth Century-
Fox Film Corporation 53tr (b (left)), 53tr (b (right)), 105bl, Walt Disney
Pictures 53br, Waterbury Films / Cinema Center Films 36tr; **TopFoto:**
ACullsteinbild 94tl, Roger-Viollet 51c, Topham Picturepoint 37cl

Cover images: *Front:* **Pearson Education Ltd:** Jon Barlow

Illustrated by Kathy Baxendale (13, 16, 30, 89, 103, 107), James
Elston (5, 31, 54, 86), Niall Harding (7, 72), Simon Jardine (46), Julian
Mosedale (18, 75), Alan Rowe (15, 19, 24, 25, 26, 27, 39, 49, 63, 64,
66, 73, 77, 87, 97, 98, 99, 100, 104), Eric Smith (3, 5, 17, 19, 29, 33, 41,
55, 57, 65, 81, 89, 110, 111), Ben Swift (9, 15, 17, 62, 70, 96), Anthony
Trimmer (26, 38, 50, 75).